Inspire a Nation:

Barack Obama's Most Electrifying
Speeches From Day One of His
Campaign Through His Inauguration

Dedicated to Guy for always —*always*—being there.

Special thanks to Raoul Heinze for his determination and editorial insights.

Edited by Jaclyn Easton
Typography Consultant: Kirk Lamb, Kirk Lamb Graphic Design
Compilation © 2009 Publishing 180
Editor's Notes © 2009 Publishing 180
ISBN: 978-0-9821005-3-0

TABLE OF CONTENTS

Editor's note: A week before his inauguration, President-Elect Barack Obama was asked by a major magazine what he most wanted for his children. He responded by sharing a letter he recently wrote to his daughters Malia, age 10 and Sasha, age 7.

We have included it here, in the beginning of this compilation of speeches, because we believe this letter reveals the emotional and motivational framework that fueled Obama from Day One of his campaign. For authenticity it was typeset using a typeface replica of his handwriting.

Dear Malia and Sasha,

I know that you've both had a lot of fun these last two years on the campaign trail, going to picnics and parades and state fairs, eating all sorts of junk food your mother and I probably shouldn't have let you have. But I also know that it hasn't always been easy for you and Mom, and that as excited as you both are about that new puppy, it doesn't make up for all the time we've been apart. I know how much I've missed these past two years, and today I want to tell you a little more about why I decided to take our family on this journey.

When I was a young man, I thought life

was all about me- about how I'd make my
way in the world, become successful, and get
the things I want. But then the two of you
came into my world with all your curiosity
and mischief and those smiles that never
fail to fill my heart and light up my day.
And suddenly, all my big plans for myself
didn't seem so important anymore. I soon
found that the greatest joy in my life was
the joy I saw in yours. And I realized that
my own life wouldn't count for much
unless I was able to ensure that you had
every opportunity for happiness and
fulfillment in yours. In the end, girls, that's
why I ran for President: because of what I
want for you and for every child in this
nation.

    I want all our children to go to schools
worthy of their potential—schools that
challenge them, inspire them, and instill in
them a sense of wonder about the world
around them. I want them to have the
chance to go to college—even if their parents
aren't rich. And I want them to get good jobs:
jobs that pay well and give them benefits like
health care, jobs that let them spend time

with their own kids and retire with dignity.

I want us to push the boundaries of discovery so that you'll live to see new technologies and inventions that improve our lives and make our planet cleaner and safer. And I want us to push our own human boundaries to reach beyond the divides of race and region, gender and religion that keep us from seeing the best in each other.

Sometimes we have to send our young men and women into war and other dangerous situations to protect our country—but when we do, I want to make sure that it is only for a very good reason, that we try our best to settle our differences with others peacefully, and that we do everything possible to keep our servicemen and women safe. And I want every child to understand that the blessings these brave Americans fight for are not free—that with the great privilege of being a citizen of this nation comes great responsibility.

That was the lesson your grandmother tried to teach me when I was your age, reading me the opening lines of the Declaration of Independence and telling me about the men and women who marched for equality because they believed those words put to paper two centuries ago should mean something.

She helped me understand that America is great not because it is perfect but because it can always be made better—and that the unfinished work of perfecting our union falls to each of us. It's a charge we pass on to our children, coming closer with each new generation to what we know America should be.

I hope both of you will take up that work, righting the wrongs that you see and working to give others the chances you've had. Not just because you have an obligation to give something back to this country that has given our family so much—although you do have that obligation. But because you have an obligation to yourself. Because it is only when you hitch your wagon to something larger than yourself that you will realize your true potential.

These are the things I want for you, to grow up in a world with no limits on your dreams and no achievements beyond your reach, and to grow into compassionate, committed women who will help build that world. And I want every child to have the same chances to learn and dream and grow and thrive that you girls have. That's why I've taken our family on this great adventure.

I am so proud of both of you. I love you more than you can ever know. And I am grateful every day for your patience, poise, grace, and humor as we prepare to start our new life together in the White House.

Love, Dad

Obama's Announcement for President
Springfield, IL
February 10, 2007

Let me begin by saying thanks to all you who've traveled, from far and wide, to brave the cold today.

We all made this journey for a reason. It's humbling, but in my heart I know you didn't come here just for me, you came here because you believe in what this country can be. In the face of war, you believe there can be peace. In the face of despair, you believe there can be hope. In the face of a politics that's shut you out, that's told you to settle, that's divided us for too long, you believe we can be one people, reaching for what's possible, building that more perfect union.

That's the journey we're on today. But let me tell you how I came to be here. As most of you know, I am not a native of this great state. I moved to Illinois over two decades ago. I was a young man then, just a year out of college; I knew no one in Chicago, was without money or family connections. But a group of churches had offered me a job as a community organizer for $13,000 a year. And I accepted the job, sight unseen, motivated then by a single, simple, powerful idea - that I might play a small part in building a better America.

My work took me to some of Chicago's poorest neighborhoods. I joined with pastors and lay-people to deal with communities that had been ravaged by plant closings. I saw that the problems people faced weren't simply local in nature - that the decision to close a steel mill was made by distant executives; that the lack of textbooks and computers in schools could be traced to the skewed priorities of politicians a thousand miles away; and that when a child turns to violence, there's a hole in his heart no government alone can fill.

It was in these neighborhoods that I received the best education I ever had, and where I learned the true meaning of my Christian faith.

After three years of this work, I went to law school, because I wanted to understand how the law should work for those in need. I became a civil rights lawyer, and taught constitutional law, and after a time, I came to understand that our cherished rights of liberty and equality depend on the active participation of an awakened electorate. It was with these ideas in mind that I arrived in this capital city as a state Senator.

It was here, in Springfield, where I saw all that is America converge - farmers and teachers, businessmen and laborers, all of them with a story to tell, all of them seeking a seat at the table, all of them clamoring to be heard. I made lasting friendships here - friends that I see in the audience today.

It was here we learned to disagree without being disagreeable - that it's possible to compromise so long as you know those principles that can never be compromised; and that so long as we're willing to listen to each other, we can assume the best in people instead of the worst.

That's why we were able to reform a death penalty system that was broken. That's why we were able to give health insurance to children in need. That's why we made the tax system more fair and just for working families, and that's why we passed ethics reforms that the cynics said could never, ever be passed.

It was here, in Springfield, where North, South, East and West come together that I was reminded of the essential decency of the American people - where I came to believe that through this decency, we can build a more hopeful America.

And that is why, in the shadow of the Old State Capitol, where Lincoln once called on a divided house to stand together, where common hopes and common dreams still, I stand before you today to announce my candidacy for President of the United States.

I recognize there is a certain presumptuousness - a certain audacity - to this announcement. I know I haven't spent a lot of time learning the ways of Washington. But I've been there long enough to know that the ways of Washington must change.

The genius of our founders is that they designed a system of government that can be changed. And we should take heart, because we've changed this country before. In the face of tyranny, a band of patriots brought an Empire to its knees. In the face of secession, we unified a nation and set the captives free. In the face of Depression, we put people back to work and lifted millions out of poverty. We welcomed immigrants to our shores, we opened railroads to the west, we landed a man on the moon, and we heard a King's call to let justice roll down like water, and righteousness like a mighty stream.

Each and every time, a new generation has risen up and done

what's needed to be done. Today we are called once more - and it is time for our generation to answer that call.

For that is our unyielding faith - that in the face of impossible odds, people who love their country can change it.

That's what Abraham Lincoln understood. He had his doubts. He had his defeats. He had his setbacks. But through his will and his words, he moved a nation and helped free a people. It is because of the millions who rallied to his cause that we are no longer divided, North and South, slave and free. It is because men and women of every race, from every walk of life, continued to march for freedom long after Lincoln was laid to rest, that today we have the chance to face the challenges of this millennium together, as one people - as Americans.

All of us know what those challenges are today - a war with no end, a dependence on oil that threatens our future, schools where too many children aren't learning, and families struggling paycheck to paycheck despite working as hard as they can. We know the challenges. We've heard them. We've talked about them for years.

What's stopped us from meeting these challenges is not the absence of sound policies and sensible plans. What's stopped us is the failure of leadership, the smallness of our politics - the ease with which we're distracted by the petty and trivial, our chronic avoidance of tough decisions, our preference for scoring cheap political points instead of rolling up our sleeves and building a working consensus to tackle big problems.

For the last six years we've been told that our mounting debts don't matter, we've been told that the anxiety Americans feel about rising health care costs and stagnant wages are an illusion, we've been told that climate change is a hoax, and that tough talk and an ill-conceived war can replace diplomacy, and strategy, and foresight. And when all else fails, when Katrina happens, or the death toll in Iraq mounts, we've been told that our crises are somebody else's fault. We're distracted from our real failures, and told to blame the other party, or gay people, or immigrants.

And as people have looked away in disillusionment and frustration, we know what's filled the void. The cynics, and the lobbyists, and the special interests who've turned our government into a game only they can afford to play. They write the checks and you get stuck with the bills, they get the access while you get to write a letter, they think they own this government, but we're here today to take it back. The time for that politics is over. It's time to turn the page.

We've made some progress already. I was proud to help lead the fight in Congress that led to the most sweeping ethics reform since Watergate.

But Washington has a long way to go. And it won't be easy. That's why we'll have to set priorities. We'll have to make hard choices. And although government will play a crucial role in bringing about the changes we need, more money and programs alone will not get us where we need to go. Each of us, in our own lives, will have to accept responsibility - for instilling an ethic of achievement in our children, for adapting to a more competitive economy, for strengthening our communities, and sharing some measure of sacrifice. So let us begin. Let us begin this hard work together. Let us transform this nation.

Let us be the generation that reshapes our economy to compete in the digital age. Let's set high standards for our schools and give them the resources they need to succeed. Let's recruit a new army of teachers, and give them better pay and more support in exchange for more accountability. Let's make college more affordable, and let's invest in scientific research, and let's lay down broadband lines through the heart of inner cities and rural towns all across America.

And as our economy changes, let's be the generation that ensures our nation's workers are sharing in our prosperity. Let's protect the hard-earned benefits their companies have promised. Let's make it possible for hardworking Americans to save for retirement. And let's allow our unions and their organizers to lift up this country's middle-class again.

Let's be the generation that ends poverty in America. Every single person willing to work should be able to get job training that leads to a job, and earn a living wage that can pay the bills, and afford child care so their kids have a safe place to go when they work. Let's do this.

Let's be the generation that finally tackles our health care crisis. We can control costs by focusing on prevention, by providing better treatment to the chronically ill, and using technology to cut the bureaucracy. Let's be the generation that says right here, right now, that we will have universal health care in America by the end of the next president's first term.

Let's be the generation that finally frees America from the tyranny of oil. We can harness homegrown, alternative fuels like ethanol and spur the production of more fuel-efficient cars. We can set up a system for capping greenhouse gases. We can turn this crisis of global warming into a moment of opportunity for innovation, and job creation, and an incentive for businesses that will serve as a model for the world. Let's be the generation that makes future generations proud of what we did here.

Most of all, let's be the generation that never forgets what happened on that September day and confront the terrorists with everything we've got. Politics doesn't have to divide us on this anymore - we can work together to keep our country safe. I've worked with Republican Senator Dick Lugar to pass a law that will secure and destroy some of the world's deadliest, unguarded weapons. We can work together to track terrorists down with a stronger military, we can tighten the net around their finances, and we can improve our intelligence capabilities. But let us also understand that ultimate victory against our enemies will come only by rebuilding our alliances and exporting those ideals that bring hope and opportunity to millions around the globe.

But all of this cannot come to pass until we bring an end to this war in Iraq. Most of you know I opposed this war from the start. I thought it was a tragic mistake. Today we grieve for the families who have lost loved ones, the hearts that have been broken, and the young lives that could have been. America, it's time to start bringing our troops home. It's time to admit that no amount of American lives can resolve the political disagreement that lies at the heart of someone else's civil war. That's why I have a plan that will bring our combat troops home by March of 2008. Letting the Iraqis know that we will not be there forever is our last, best hope to pressure the Sunni and Shia to come to the table and find peace.

Finally, there is one other thing that is not too late to get right about this war - and that is the homecoming of the men and women - our veterans - who have sacrificed the most. Let us honor their valor by providing the care they need and rebuilding the military they love. Let us be the generation that begins this work.

I know there are those who don't believe we can do all these things. I understand the skepticism. After all, every four years, candidates from both parties make similar promises, and I expect this year will be no different. All of us running for president will travel around the country offering ten-point plans and making grand speeches; all of us will trumpet those qualities we believe make us uniquely qualified to lead the country. But too many times, after the election is over, and the confetti is swept away, all those promises fade from memory, and the lobbyists and the special interests move in, and people turn away, disappointed as before, left to struggle on their own.

That is why this campaign can't only be about me. It must be about us - it must be about what we can do together. This campaign must be the occasion, the vehicle, of your hopes, and your dreams. It will take your time, your energy, and your advice - to push us forward when we're doing right, and to let us know when we're not. This campaign has to be about reclaiming the meaning of citizenship, restoring our sense of common purpose, and realizing that few obstacles can withstand the power of millions of voices calling for change.

By ourselves, this change will not happen. Divided, we are bound to fail.

But the life of a tall, gangly, self-made Springfield lawyer tells us that a different future is possible.

He tells us that there is power in words.

He tells us that there is power in conviction.

That beneath all the differences of race and region, faith and station, we are one people.

He tells us that there is power in hope.

As Lincoln organized the forces arrayed against slavery, he was heard to say: "Of strange, discordant, and even hostile elements, we gathered from the four winds, and formed and fought to battle through."

That is our purpose here today.

That's why I'm in this race.

Not just to hold an office, but to gather with you to transform a nation.

I want to win that next battle - for justice and opportunity.

I want to win that next battle - for better schools, and better jobs, and health care for all.

I want us to take up the unfinished business of perfecting our union, and building a better America.

And if you will join me in this improbable quest, if you feel destiny calling, and see as I see, a future of endless possibility stretching before us; if you sense, as I sense, that the time is now to shake off our slumber, and slough off our fear, and make good on the debt we owe past and future generations, then I'm ready to take up the cause, and march with you, and work with you. Together, starting today, let us finish the work that needs to be done, and usher in a new birth of freedom on this Earth.

California State Democratic Convention
San Diego, CA
May 2, 2007

It has now been a little over two months since we began this campaign. In that time we have traveled all across this country. And before every event we do, I usually have a minute to sit quietly and collect my thoughts. And recently, I've found myself reflecting on what it was that led me to public service in the first place.

I live in Chicago now, but I am not a native of that great city. I moved there when I was just a year out of college, and a group of churches offered me a job as a community organizer so I could help rebuild neighborhoods that had been devastated by the closing of steel plants.

The salary was $12,000 a year plus enough money to buy an old, beat-up car, and so I took the job and drove out to Chicago, where I didn't know a soul. And during the time I was there, we worked to set up job training programs for the unemployed and after school programs for kids.

And it was the best education I ever had, because I learned in those neighborhoods that when ordinary people come together, they can achieve extraordinary things.

After three years, I went back to law school. I left there with a degree and a lifetime of debt, but I turned down the corporate job offers so I could come back to Chicago and organize a voter registration drive. I also started a civil rights practice, and began to teach constitutional law.

And after a few years, people started coming up to me and telling me I should run for state Senate. So I did what every man does when he's faced with a big decision - I prayed, and I asked my wife. And after consulting those two higher powers, I decided to get in the race.

And everywhere I'd go, I'd get two questions. First, they'd ask, "Where'd you get that funny name, Barack Obama?" Because people just couldn't pronounce it. They'd call me "Alabama," or they'd call me "Yo Mama." And I'd tell them that my father was from Kenya, and that's where I got my name. And my mother was from Kansas, and that's where I got my accent from.

And the second thing people would ask me was, "You seem like a nice young man. You've done all this great work. You've been a community organizer, and you teach law school, you're a civil rights attorney, you're a family man - why would you wanna go into something dirty and nasty like politics?"

And I understand the question, and the cynicism. We all understand it.

We understand it because we get the sense today that politics has become a business and not a mission. In the last several years, we have seen Washington become a place where keeping score of who's up and who's down is more important than who's working on behalf of the American people.

We have been told that our mounting debts don't matter, that the economy is doing great, and so Americans should be left to face their anxiety about rising health care costs and disappearing pensions on their own.

We've been told that climate change is a hoax, that our broken schools cannot be fixed, that we are destined to send millions of dollars a day to Mideast dictators for their oil. And we've seen how a foreign policy based on bluster and bombast can lead us into a war that should've never been authorized and never been waged.

And when we try to have an honest debate about the crises we face, whether it's on the Senate floor or a Sunday talk show, the conversation isn't about finding common ground, it's about finding someone to blame. We're divided into Red States and Blue States, and told to always point the finger at somebody else - the other party, or gay people, or immigrants.

For good reason, the rest of us have become cynical about what politics can achieve in this country, and as we've turned away in frustration, we know what's filled the void. The lobbyists and influence-peddlers with the cash and the connections - the ones who've turned government into a game only they can afford to play. They write the checks and you get stuck with the bills, they get the access while you get to write a letter, they think they own this government, but we're here to tell them it's not for sale.

People tell me I haven't spent a lot of time learning the ways of Washington. But I promise you this - I've been there long enough to know that the ways of Washington must change.

I'm running for President because the time for the can't-do, won't-do, won't-even-try style of politics is over. It's time to turn the page.

There is an awakening taking place in America today. From New Hampshire to California, from Texas to Iowa, we are seeing crowds we've never seen before; we're seeing people showing up to the very first political event of their lives.

They're coming because they know we are at a crossroads right now. Because we are facing a set of challenges we haven't seen in a generation - and if we don't meet those challenges, we could end up leaving our children a world that's a little poorer and a little meaner than we found it.

And so the American people are hungry for a different kind of politics - the kind of politics based on the ideals this country was founded upon. The idea that we are all connected as one people. That we all have a stake in one another.

It's what I learned as a state Senator in Illinois. That you can turn the page on old debates; that it's possible to compromise so long as you as you never compromise your principles; and that so long as we're willing to listen to each other, we can assume the best in people instead of the worst.

That's how we were able to reform a death penalty system that sent 13 innocent people to death row. That's how we were able to give health insurance to 20,000 more children who needed it. That's how we gave $100 million worth of tax cuts to working families in Illinois.

And that's how we passed the first ethics reform in twenty-five years.

We have seen too many campaigns where our problems are talked to death. Where ten-point plans are crushed under the weight of the same old politics once the election's over. Where experience in Washington doesn't always translate to results for the American people.

And so if we do not change our politics - if we do not fundamentally change the way Washington works - then the problems we've been talking about for the last generation will be the same ones that haunt us for generations to come.

We must find a way to come together in this country - to realize that the responsibility we have to one another as Americans is greater than the pursuit of any ideological agenda or corporate bottom line.

Democrats of California, it's time to turn the page.

It's time to turn the page on health care - to bring together unions and businesses, Democrats and Republicans, and to let the insurance and drug companies know that while they get a seat at the table, they don't get to buy every chair.

When I am president, I will sign a universal health care law by the end of my first term. My plan will cover the uninsured by letting people buy into the same kind of health care plan that members of Congress give themselves. It will bring down costs by investing in information technology, and preventative care, and by stopping the drug companies from price-gouging when patients need their medicine. It will help business and families shoulder the burden of catastrophic care so that an illness doesn't lead to a bankruptcy. And it will save the average family a thousand dollars a year on their premiums. We can do this.

It's time to turn the page on education - to move past the slow decay of indifference that says some schools can't be fixed and some kids just can't learn.

As President, I will launch a campaign to recruit and support hundreds of thousands of new teachers across the country, because the most important part of any education is the person standing in the front of the classroom. It's time to treat teaching like the profession it is - paying teachers what they deserve and working with them - not against them - to develop the high standards we need. We can do this.

It's time to turn the page on energy - to break the political stalemate that's kept our fuel efficiency standards in the same place for twenty years; to tell the oil and auto industries that they must act, not only because their future's at stake, but because the future of our country and our planet is at stake as well.

As President, I will institute a cap-and-trade system that would dramatically reduce carbon emissions and auction off emissions credits that would generate millions of dollars to invest in renewable sources of energy. I'll put in place a low-carbon fuel standard like you have here in California that will take 32 million cars' worth of pollution off the road. And I'd raise the fuel efficiency standards for our cars and trucks because we know we have the technology to do it and it's time we did. We can do this.

We can do all of this. But most of all, we have to turn the page on this disaster in Iraq and restore our standing in the world.

I am proud that I stood up in 2002 and urged our leaders not to take us down this dangerous path. And so many of you did the same, even when it wasn't popular to do so.

We knew back then this war was a mistake. We knew back then that it was dangerous diversion from the struggle against the terrorists who attacked us on September 11th. We knew back then that we could find ourselves in an occupation of undetermined length, at undetermined cost, with undetermined consequences.

But the war went forward. And now, we've seen those consequences and we mourn for the dead and wounded.

I was in New Hampshire the other week when a woman told me that her nephew was leaving for Iraq. And as she started telling me how much she'd miss him and how worried she was about him, she began to cry. And she said to me, "I can't breathe. I want to know, when am I going to be able to breathe again?"

It is time to let this woman know she can breathe again. It is time to put an end this war.

The majority of both houses of the American Congress - Republicans and Democrats - just passed a bill that would do exactly that. It's a bill similar to the plan I introduced in January that says there is no military solution to this civil war - that the last, best hope to pressure the warring factions to reach a political settlement is to let the Iraqi government know that America will not be there forever - to begin a phased withdrawal with the goal of bringing all combat brigades home by March 31st, 2008.

We are one signature away from ending this war. If the President refuses to sign it, we will go back and find the sixteen votes we need to end this war without him. We will turn up the pressure on all those Republican Congressmen and Senators who refuse to acknowledge the reality that the American people know so well, and we will get this done. We will bring our troops home. It's time to turn the page.

It's time to show the world that America is still the last, best hope of Earth. This President may occupy the White House, but for the last six years the position of leader of the free world has remained open.

It's time to fill that role once more. Whether it's terrorism or climate change, global AIDS or the spread of weapons of mass destruction, America cannot meet the threats of this new century alone, but the world cannot meet them without America. It's time for us to lead.

It's time for us to show the world that we are not a country that ships prisoners in the dead of night to be tortured in far off countries. That we are not a country that runs prisons which lock people away without ever telling them why they are there or what they are charged with. We are not a country which preaches compassion to others while we allow bodies to float down the streets of a major American city.

That is not who we are.

We are America. We are the nation that liberated a continent from a madman, that lifted ourselves from the depths of Depression, that won Civil Rights, and Women's Rights, and Voting Rights for all our people. We are the beacon that has led generations of weary travelers to find opportunity, and liberty, and hope on our doorstep. That's who we are.

I was down in Selma, Alabama awhile back, and we were celebrating the 42nd anniversary of the march across the Edmund Pettus Bridge. It was a march of ordinary Americans - maids and cooks, preachers and Pullman porters who faced down fire hoses and dogs, tear gas and billy clubs when they tried to get to the other side. But every time they were stopped, every time they were knocked down, they got back up, they came back, and they kept on marching. And finally they crossed over. It was called Bloody Sunday, and it was the culmination of the Civil Rights Movement.

When I came back from that celebration, people would say, oh, what a wonderful celebration of African-American history that must have been. And I would say, no, that wasn't African-American history. That was a celebration of American history - it's our story.

And it reminds us of a simple truth - a truth I learned all those years ago as an organizer in Chicago - a truth you carry by being here today - that in the face of impossible odds, people who love their country can change it.

I am confident about my ability to lead this country. But I also know that I can't do it without you. There will be times when I get tired, there will be times when I make a mistake - it's true, talk to my wife, she'll tell you. But this campaign that we're running has to be about your hopes, and your dreams, and what you will do. Because there are few obstacles that can withstand the power of millions of voices calling for change.

That's how change has always happened - not from the top-down, but from the bottom-up.

And that's exactly how you and I will change this country.

California, if you want a new kind of politics, it's time to turn the page.

If you want an end to the old divisions, and the stale debates, and the score-keeping and the name-calling, it's time to turn the page.

If you want health care for every American and a world-class education for all our children; if you want energy independence and an end to this war in Iraq; if you believe America is still that last, best hope of Earth, then it's time to turn the page.

It's time to turn the page for hope. It's time to turn the page for justice. It is time to turn the page and write the next chapter in the great American story. Let's begin the work. Let's do this together. Let's turn that page. Thank you.

Iowa Caucus Night
Des Moines, Iowa
January 03, 2008

Thank you, Iowa.

You know, they said this day would never come.

They said our sights were set too high.

They said this country was too divided; too disillusioned to ever come together around a common purpose.

But on this January night - at this defining moment in history - you have done what the cynics said we couldn't do. You have done what the state of New Hampshire can do in five days. You have done what America can do in this New Year, 2008. In lines that stretched around schools and churches; in small towns and big cities; you came together as Democrats, Republicans and Independents to stand up and say that we are one nation; we are one people; and our time for change has come.

You said the time has come to move beyond the bitterness and pettiness and anger that's consumed Washington; to end the political strategy that's been all about division and instead make it about addition - to build a coalition for change that stretches through Red States and Blue States. Because that's how we'll win in November, and that's how we'll finally meet the challenges that we face as a nation.

We are choosing hope over fear. We're choosing unity over division, and sending a powerful message that change is coming to

America.

You said the time has come to tell the lobbyists who think their money and their influence speak louder than our voices that they don't own this government, we do; and we are here to take it back.

The time has come for a President who will be honest about the choices and the challenges we face; who will listen to you and learn from you even when we disagree; who won't just tell you what you want to hear, but what you need to know. And in New Hampshire, if you give me the same chance that Iowa did tonight, I will be that president for America.

Thank you.

I'll be a President who finally makes health care affordable and available to every single American the same way I expanded health care in Illinois – by bringing Democrats and Republicans together to get the job done.

I'll be a President who ends the tax breaks for companies that ship our jobs overseas and put a middle-class tax cut into the pockets of the working Americans who deserve it.

I'll be a President who harnesses the ingenuity of farmers and scientists and entrepreneurs to free this nation from the tyranny of oil once and for all.

And I'll be a President who ends this war in Iraq and finally brings our troops home; who restores our moral standing; who understands that 9/11 is not a way to scare up votes, but a challenge that should unite America and the world against the common threats of the twenty-first century; common threats of terrorism and nuclear weapons; climate change and poverty; genocide and disease.

Tonight, we are one step closer to that vision of America because of what you did here in Iowa. And so I'd especially like to thank the organizers and the precinct captains; the volunteers and the staff who made this all possible.

And while I'm at it, on "thank yous," I think it makes sense for me to thank the love of my life, the rock of the Obama family, the closer on the campaign trail; give it up for Michelle Obama.

I know you didn't do this for me. You did this-you did this because you believed so deeply in the most American of ideas - that in the face of impossible odds, people who love this country can change it.

 know this-I know this because while I may be standing here tonight, I'll never forget that my journey began on the streets of Chicago doing what so many of you have done for this campaign and all the campaigns here in Iowa - organizing, and working, and fighting to make people's lives just a little bit better.

I know how hard it is. It comes with little sleep, little pay, and a lot of sacrifice. There are days of disappointment, but sometimes, just sometimes, there are nights like this - a night-a night that, years from now, when we've made the changes we believe in; when more families can afford to see a doctor; when our children-when Malia and Sasha and your children-inherit a planet that's a little cleaner and safer; when the world sees America differently, and America sees itself as a nation less divided and more united; you'll be able to look back with pride and say that this was the moment when it all began.

This was the moment when the improbable beat what Washington always said was inevitable.

This was the moment when we tore down barriers that have divided us for too long - when we rallied people of all parties and ages to a common cause; when we finally gave Americans who'd never participated in politics a reason to stand up and to do so.

This was the moment when we finally beat back the politics of fear, and doubt, and cynicism; the politics where we tear each other down instead of lifting this country up. This was the moment.

Years from now, you'll look back and you'll say that this was the moment - this was the place - where America remembered what it means to hope.

For many months, we've been teased, even derided for talking about hope.

But we always knew that hope is not blind optimism. It's not ignoring the enormity of the task ahead or the roadblocks that stand in our path. It's not sitting on the sidelines or shirking from a fight. Hope is that thing inside us that insists, despite all evidence to the contrary, that something better awaits us if we have the courage to reach for it, and to work for it, and to fight for it.

Hope is what I saw in the eyes of the young woman in Cedar Rapids who works the night shift after a full day of college and still can't afford health care for a sister who's ill; a young woman who still believes that this country will give her the chance to live out her dreams.

Hope is what I heard in the voice of the New Hampshire woman who told me that she hasn't been able to breathe since her nephew left for Iraq; who still goes to bed each night praying for his safe return.

Hope is what led a band of colonists to rise up against an empire; what led the greatest of generations to free a continent and heal a nation; what led young women and young men to sit at lunch counters and brave fire hoses and march through Selma and Montgomery for freedom's cause.

Hope-hope-is what led me here today - with a father from Kenya; a mother from Kansas; and a story that could only happen in the United States of America. Hope is the bedrock of this nation; the belief that our destiny will not be written for us, but by us; by all those men and women who are not content to settle for the world as it is; who have the courage to remake the world as it should be.

That is what we started here in Iowa, and that is the message we can now carry to New Hampshire and beyond; the same message we had when we were up and when we were down; the one that can change this country brick by brick, block by block, calloused hand by calloused hand - that together, ordinary people can do extraordinary things; because we are not a collection of Red States and Blue States, we are the United States of America; and at this moment, in this election, we are ready to believe again. Thank you, Iowa.

Super Tuesday
Chicago, IL
February 5, 2008

Before I begin, I just want to send my condolences to the victims of the storms that hit Tennessee and Arkansas. They are in our thoughts and in our prayers.

Well, the polls are just closing in California and the votes are still being counted in cities and towns across the country. But there is one thing on this February night that we do not need the final results to know - our time has come, our movement is real, and change is coming to America.

Only a few hundred miles from here, almost one year ago to the day, we stood on the steps of the Old State Capitol to reaffirm a truth that was spoken there so many generations ago - that a house divided cannot stand; that we are more than a collection of Red States and Blue States; we are, and always will be, the United States of America.

What began as a whisper in Springfield soon carried across the corn fields of Iowa, where farmers and factory workers; students and seniors stood up in numbers we've never seen. They stood up to say that maybe this year, we don't have to settle for a politics where scoring points is more important than solving problems. This time we can finally do something about health care we can't afford or mortgages we can't pay. This time can be different.

Their voices echoed from the hills of New Hampshire to the

deserts of Nevada, where teachers and cooks and kitchen workers stood up to say that maybe Washington doesn't have to be run by lobbyists anymore. They reached the coast of South Carolina when people said that maybe we don't have to be divided by race and region and gender; that crumbling schools are stealing the future of black children and white children; that we can come together and build an America that gives every child, everywhere the opportunity to live their dreams. This time can be different.

And today, on this Tuesday in February, in states North and South, East and West, what began as a whisper in Springfield has swelled to a chorus of millions calling for change. A chorus that cannot be ignored. That cannot be deterred. This time can be different because this campaign for the presidency is different.

It's different not because of me, but because of you. Because you are tired of being disappointed and tired of being let down. You're tired of hearing promises made and plans proposed in the heat of a campaign only to have nothing change when everyone goes back to Washington. Because the lobbyists just write another check. Or because politicians start worrying about how they'll win the next election instead of why they should. Or because they focus on who's up and who's down instead of who matters.

And while Washington is consumed with the same drama and division and distraction, another family puts up a For Sale sign in the front yard. Another factory shuts its doors. Another soldier waves goodbye as he leaves on another tour of duty in a war that should've never been authorized and never been waged. It goes on and on and on.

But in this election - at this moment - you are standing up all across this country to say, not this time. Not this year. The stakes are too high and the challenges too great to play the same Washington game with the same Washington players and expect a different result. This time must be different.

Now, this isn't about me and it's not about Senator Clinton. As I've said before, she was a friend before this campaign and she'll be a friend after it's over. I respect her as a colleague, and I congratulate her on her victories tonight.

But this fall we owe the American people a real choice. It's change versus more of the same. It's the future versus the past.

It's a choice between going into this election with Republicans and Independents already united against us, or going against their nominee with a campaign that has united Americans of all parties around a common purpose.

It's a choice between having a debate with the other party about who has the most experience in Washington, or having one about who's most likely to change Washington. Because that's a debate we can win.

It's a choice between a candidate who's taken more money from Washington lobbyists than either Republican in this race, and a campaign that hasn't taken a dime of their money because we've been funded by you.

And if I am your nominee, my opponent will not be able to say that I voted for the war in Iraq; or that I gave George Bush the benefit of the doubt on Iran; or that I support the Bush-Cheney policy of not talking to leaders we don't like. And he will not be able to say that I wavered on something as fundamental as whether or not it's ok for America to use torture - because it is never ok. That is the choice in this election.

The Republicans running for President have already tied themselves to the past. They speak of a hundred year war in Iraq and billions more on tax breaks for the wealthiest few who don't need them and didn't ask for them - tax breaks that mortgage our children's future on a mountain of debt at a time when there are families who can't pay their medical bills and students who can't pay their tuition.

They are running on the politics of yesterday, and that is why our party must be the party of tomorrow. And that is the party I will lead as President.

I'll be the President who ends the tax breaks to companies that ship our jobs overseas and start putting them in the pockets of working Americans who deserve it. And struggling homeowners. And seniors who should retire with dignity and respect.

I'll be the President who finally brings Democrats and Republicans together to make health care affordable and available for every single American. We will put a college education within reach of anyone who wants to go, and instead of just talking about how great our teachers are, we will reward them for their greatness, with more pay and better support. And we will harnesses the ingenuity of farmers and scientists and entrepreneurs to free this nation from the tyranny of oil once and for all.

And when I am President, we will put an end to a politics that uses 9/11 as a way to scare up votes, and start seeing it as a challenge that should unite America and the world against the common threats of the twenty-first century: terrorism and nuclear weapons; climate change and poverty; genocide and disease.

We can do this. It will not be easy. It will require struggle and sacrifice. There will setbacks and we will make mistakes. And that is why we need all the help we can get. So tonight I want to speak directly to all those Americans who have yet to join this movement but still hunger for change - we need you. We need you to stand with us, and work with us, and help us prove that together, ordinary people can still do extraordinary things.

I am blessed to be standing in the city where my own extraordinary journey began. A few miles from here, in the shadow of a shuttered steel plant, is where I learned what it takes to make change happen.

I was a young organizer then, intent on fighting joblessness and poverty on the South Side, and I still remember one of the very first meetings I put together. We had worked on it for days, but no one showed up. Our volunteers felt so defeated, they wanted to quit. And to be honest, so did I.

But at that moment, I looked outside and saw some young boys tossing stones at a boarded-up apartment building across the street. They were like boys in so many cities across the country - boys without prospects, without guidance, without hope. And I turned to the volunteers, and I asked them, "Before you quit, I want you to answer one question. What will happen to those boys?" And the volunteers looked out that window, and they decided that night to keep going - to keep organizing, keep fighting for better schools, and better jobs, and better health care. And so did I. And slowly, but surely, in the weeks and months to come, the community began to change.

You see, the challenges we face will not be solved with one meeting in one night. Change will not come if we wait for some other person or some other time.

We are the ones we've been waiting for. We are the change that we seek. We are the hope of those boys who have little; who've been told that they cannot have what they dream; that they cannot be what they imagine.

Yes they can.

We are the hope of the father who goes to work before dawn and lies awake with doubts that tell him he cannot give his children the same opportunities that someone gave him.

Yes he can.

We are the hope of the woman who hears that her city will not be rebuilt; that she cannot reclaim the life that was swept away in a terrible storm.

Yes she can.

We are the hope of the future; the answer to the cynics who tell us our house must stand divided; that we cannot come together; that we cannot remake this world as it should be.

Because we know what we have seen and what we believe - that what began as a whisper has now swelled to a chorus that cannot be ignored; that will not be deterred; that will ring out across this land as a hymn that will heal this nation, repair this world, and make this time different than all the rest - Yes. We. Can.

Potomac Primary Night
Madison, WI
February 12, 2008

Today, the change we seek swept through the Chesapeake and over the Potomac.

We won the state of Maryland. We won the Commonwealth of Virginia. And though we won in Washington D.C., this movement won't stop until there's change in Washington. And tonight, we're on our way.

But we know how much farther we have to go.

We know it takes more than one night – or even one election – to overcome decades of money and the influence; bitter partisanship and petty bickering that's shut you out, let you down and told you to settle.

We know our road will not be easy.

But we also know that at this moment the cynics can no longer say our hope is false.

We have now won east and west, north and south, and across the heartland of this country we love. We have given young people a reason to believe, and brought folks back to the polls who want to believe again. And we are bringing together Democrats and Independents and Republicans; blacks and whites; Latinos and Asians; small states and big states; Red States and Blue States into a United States of America.

This is the new American majority. This is what change looks like when it happens from the bottom up. And in this election, your voices will be heard.

Because at a time when so many people are struggling to keep up with soaring costs in a sluggish economy, we know that the status quo in Washington just won't do. Not this time. Not this year. We can't keep playing the same Washington game with the same Washington players and expect a different result – because it's a game that ordinary Americans are losing.

It's a game where lobbyists write check after check and Exxon turns record profits, while you pay the price at the pump, and our planet is put at risk. That's what happens when lobbyists set the agenda, and that's why they won't drown out your voices anymore when I am President of the United States of America.

It's a game where trade deals like NAFTA ship jobs overseas and force parents to compete with their teenagers to work for minimum wage at Wal-Mart. That's what happens when the American worker doesn't have a voice at the negotiating table, when leaders change their positions on trade with the politics of the moment, and that's why we need a President who will listen to Main Street – not just Wall Street; a President who will stand with workers not just when it's easy, but when it's hard.

It's a game where Democrats and Republicans fail to come together year after year after year, while another mother goes without health care for her sick child. That's why we have to put an end to the division and distraction in Washington, so that we can unite this nation around a common purpose, a higher purpose.

It's a game where the only way for Democrats to look tough on national security is by talking, and acting and voting like Bush-McCain Republicans, while our troops are sent to fight tour after tour of duty in a war that should've never been authorized and should've never been waged. That's what happens when we use 9/11 to scare up votes, and that's why we need to do more than end a war – we need to end the mindset that got us into war.

That's the choice in this primary. It's about whether we choose to play the game, or whether we choose to end it; it's change that polls well, or change we can believe in; it's the past versus the future. And when I'm the Democratic nominee for President – that will be the choice in November.

John McCain is an American hero. We honor his service to our nation. But his priorities don't address the real problems of the American people, because they are bound to the failed policies of the past.

George Bush won't be on the ballot this November, but his war and his tax cuts for the wealthy will.

When I am the nominee, I will offer a clear choice. John McCain won't be able to say that I ever supported this war in Iraq, because I opposed it from the beginning. Senator McCain said the other day that we might be mired for a hundred years in Iraq, which is reason enough to not give him four years in the White House.

If we had chosen a different path, the right path, we could have finished the job in Afghanistan, and put more resources into the fight against bin Laden; and instead of spending hundreds of billions of dollars in Baghdad, we could have put that money into our schools and hospitals, our road and bridges – and that's what the American people need us to do right now.

And I admired Senator McCain when he stood up and said that it offended his "conscience" to support the Bush tax cuts for the wealthy in a time of war; that he couldn't support a tax cut where "so many of the benefits go to the most fortunate." But somewhere along the road to the Republican nomination, the Straight Talk Express lost its wheels, because now he's all for them.

Well I'm not. We can't keep spending money that we don't have in a war that we shouldn't have fought. We can't keep mortgaging our children's future on a mountain of debt. We can't keep driving a wider and wider gap between the few who are rich and the rest who struggle to keep pace. It's time to turn the page.

We need a new direction in this country. Everywhere I go, I meet Americans who can't wait another day for change. They're not just showing up to hear a speech – they need to know that politics can make a difference in their lives, that it's not too late to reclaim the American Dream.

It's a dream shared in big cities and small towns; across races, regions and religions – that if you work hard, you can support a family; that if you get sick, there will be health care you can afford; that you can retire with the dignity and security and respect that you have earned; that your kids can get a good education, and young people can go to college even if they're not rich. That is our common hope. That is the American Dream.

It's the dream of the father who goes to work before dawn and lies awake at night wondering how he's going to pay the bills. He needs us to restore fairness to our economy by putting a tax cut into the pockets of working people, and seniors, and struggling homeowners.

It's the dream of the woman who told me she works the night shift after a full day of college and still can't afford health care for a sister who's ill. She needs us to finally come together to make health care affordable and available for every American.

It's the dream of the senior I met who lost his pension when the company he gave his life to went bankrupt. He doesn't need bankruptcy laws that protect banks and big lenders. He needs us to protect pensions, not CEO bonuses; and to do what it takes to make sure that the American people can count on Social Security today, tomorrow and forever.

It's the dream of the teacher who works at Dunkin Donuts after school just to make ends meet. She needs better pay, and more support, and the freedom to do more than just teach to the test. And if her students want to go on to college, they shouldn't fear decades of debt. That's why I'll make college affordable with an annual $4,000 tax credit if you're willing to do community service, or national service. We will invest in you, but we'll ask you to invest in your country.

That is our calling in this campaign. To reaffirm that fundamental belief – I am my brother's keeper, I am my sister's keeper – that makes us one people, and one nation. It's time to stand up and reach for what's possible, because together, people who love their country can change it.

Now when I start talking like this, some folks tell me that I've got my head in the clouds. That I need a reality check. That we're still offering false hope. But my own story tells me that in the United States of America, there has never been anything false about hope.

I should not be here today. I was not born into money or status. I was born to a teenage mom in Hawaii, and my dad left us when I was two. But my family gave me love, they gave me education, and most of all they gave me hope – hope that in America, no dream is beyond our grasp if we reach for it, and fight for it, and work for it.

Because hope is not blind optimism. I know how hard it will be to make these changes. I know this because I fought on the streets of Chicago as a community organizer to bring jobs to the jobless in the shadow of a shuttered steel plant. I've fought in the courts as a civil rights lawyer to make sure people weren't denied their rights because of what they looked like or where they came from. I've fought in the legislature to take power away from lobbyists. I've won some of those fights, but I've lost some of them too. I've seen good legislation die because good intentions weren't backed by a mandate for change.

The politics of hope does not mean hoping things come easy. Because nothing worthwhile in this country has ever happened unless somebody, somewhere stood up when it was hard; stood up when they were told – no you can't, and said yes we can.

And where better to affirm our ideals than here in Wisconsin, where a century ago the progressive movement was born. It was rooted in the principle that the voices of the people can speak louder than special interests; that citizens can be connected to their government and to one another; and that all of us share a common destiny, an American Dream.

Yes we can reclaim that dream.

Yes we can heal this nation.

The voices of the American people have carried us a great distance on this improbable journey, but we have much further to go. Now we carry our message to farms and factories across this state, and to the cities and small towns of Ohio, to the open plains deep in the heart of Texas, and all the way to Democratic National Convention in Denver; it's the same message we had when we were up, and when were down; that out of many, we are one; that our destiny will not be written for us, but by us; and that we can cast off our doubts and fears and cynicism because our dream will not be deferred; our future will not be denied; and our time for change has come.

March 4th Primary Night
Texas and Ohio
San Antonio, TX
March 4, 2008

Well, we are in the middle of a very close race right now in Texas, and we may not even know the final results until morning. We do know that Senator Clinton has won Rhode Island, and while there are a lot of votes to be counted in Ohio, it looks like she did well there too, and so we congratulate her on those states. We also know that we have won the state of Vermont. And we know this - no matter what happens tonight, we have nearly the same delegate lead as we did this morning, and we are on our way to winning this nomination.

You know, decades ago, as a community organizer, I learned that the real work of democracy begins far from the closed doors and marbled halls of Washington.

It begins on street corners and front porches; in living rooms and meeting halls with ordinary Americans who see the world as it is and realize that we have it within our power to remake the world as it should be.

It is with that hope that we began this unlikely journey - the hope that if we could go block by block, city by city, state by state and build a movement that spanned race and region; party and gender; if we could give young people a reason to vote and the young at heart a reason to believe again; if we could inspire a nation to come together again, then we could turn the page on the politics that's shut us out, let us down, and told us to settle. We could write a new chapter in the American story.

We were told this wasn't possible. We were told the climb was too steep. We were told our country was too cynical - that we were just being naïve; that we couldn't really change the world as it is.

But then a few people in Iowa stood up to say, "Yes we can." And then a few more of you stood up from the hills of New Hampshire to the coast of South Carolina. And then a few million of you stood up from Savannah to Seattle; from Boise to Baton Rouge. And tonight, because of you - because of a movement you built that stretches from Vermont's Green Mountains to the streets of San Antonio, we can stand up with confidence and clarity to say that we are turning the page, and we are ready to write the next great chapter in America's story.

In the coming weeks, we will begin a great debate about the future of this country with a man who has served it bravely and loves it dearly. And tonight, I called John McCain and congratulated him on winning the Republican nomination.

But in this election, we will offer two very different visions of the America we see in the twenty-first century. Because John McCain may claim long history of straight talk and independent-thinking, and I respect that. But in this campaign, he's fallen in line behind the very same policies that have ill-served America. He has seen where George Bush has taken our country, and he promises to keep us on the very same course.

It's the same course that threatens a century of war in Iraq - a third and fourth and fifth tour of duty for brave troops who've done all we've asked them to, even while we ask little and expect nothing of the Iraqi government whose job it is to put their country back together. A course where we spend billions of dollars a week that could be used to rebuild our roads and our schools; to care for our veterans and send our children to college.

It's the same course that continues to divide and isolate America from the world by substituting bluster and bullying for direct diplomacy - by ignoring our allies and refusing to talk to our enemies even though Presidents from Kennedy to Reagan have done just that; because strong countries and strong leaders aren't afraid to tell hard truths to petty dictators.

And it's the same course that offers the same tired answer to workers without health care and families without homes; to students in debt and children who go to bed hungry in the richest nation on Earth - four more years of tax breaks for the biggest corporations and the wealthiest few who don't need them and aren't even asking for them. It's a course that further divides Wall Street from Main Street; where struggling families are told to pull themselves up by their bootstraps because there's nothing government can do or should do - and so we should give more to those with the most and let the chips fall where they may.

Well we are here tonight to say that this is not the America we believe in and this is not the future we want. We want a new course for this country. We want new leadership in Washington. We want change in America.

John McCain and Senator Clinton echo each other in dismissing this call for change. They say it is eloquent but empty; speeches and not solutions. And yet, they should know that it's a call that did not begin with my words. It began with words that were spoken on the floors of factories in Ohio and across the deep plains of Texas; words that came from classrooms in South Carolina and living rooms in the state of Iowa; from first-time voters and life-long cynics; from Democrats and Republicans alike.

They should know that there's nothing empty about the call for affordable health care that came from the young student who told me she gets three hours of sleep because she works the night shift after a full day of college and still can't pay her sister's medical bills.

There's nothing empty about the call for help that came from the mother in San Antonio who saw her mortgage double in two weeks and didn't know where her two-year olds would sleep at night when they were kicked out of their home.

There's nothing empty about the call for change that came from the elderly woman who wants it so badly that she sent me an envelope with a money order for $3.01 and a simple verse of scripture tucked inside.

These Americans know that government cannot solve all of our problems, and they don't expect it to. Americans know that we have to work harder and study more to compete in a global economy. We know that we need to take responsibility for ourselves and our children - that we need to spend more time with them, and teach them well, and put a book in their hands instead of a video game once in awhile. We know this.

But we also believe that there is a larger responsibility we have to one another as Americans.

We believe that we rise or fall as one nation - as one people. That we are our brother's keeper. That we are our sister's keeper.

We believe that a child born tonight should have the same chances whether she arrives in the barrios of San Antonio or the suburbs of St. Louis; on the streets of Chicago or the hills of Appalachia.

We believe that when she goes to school for the first time, it should be in a place where the rats don't outnumber the computers; that when she applies to college, cost is no barrier to a degree that will allow her to compete with children in China or India for the jobs of the twenty-first century.

We believe that these jobs should provide wages that can raise her family, health care for when she gets sick and a pension for when she retires.

We believe that when she tucks her own children into bed, she should feel safe knowing that they are protected from the threats we face by the bravest, best-equipped, military in the world, led by a Commander-in-Chief who has the judgment to know when to send them into battle and which battlefield to fight on.

And if that child should ever get the chance to travel the world, and someone should ask her where she is from, we believe that she should always be able to hold her head high with pride in her voice when she answers "I am an American."

That is the course we seek. That is the change we are calling for. You can call it many things, but you cannot call it empty.

If I am the nominee of this party, I will not allow us to be distracted by the same politics that seeks to divide us with false charges and meaningless labels. In this campaign, we will not stand for the politics that uses religion as a wedge, and patriotism as a bludgeon.

I owe what I am to this country I love, and I will never forget it. Where else could a young man who grew up herding goats in Kenya get the chance to fulfill his dream of a college education? Where else could he marry a white girl from Kansas whose parents survived war and depression to find opportunity out west? Where else could they have a child who would one day have the chance to run for the highest office in the greatest nation the world has ever known? Where else, but in the United States of America?

It is now my hope and our task to set this country on a course that will keep this promise alive in the twenty-first century. And the eyes of the world are watching to see if we can.

There is a young man on my campaign whose grandfather lives in Uganda. He is 81 years old and has never experienced true democracy in his lifetime. During the reign of Idi Amin, he was literally hunted and the only reason he escaped was thanks to the kindness of others and a few good-sized trunks. And on the night of the Iowa caucuses, that 81-year-old man stayed up until five in the morning, huddled by his television, waiting for the results.

The world is watching what we do here. The world is paying attention to how we conduct ourselves. What will we they see? What will we tell them? What will we show them?

Can we come together across party and region; race and religion to restore prosperity and opportunity as the birthright of every American?

Can we lead the community of nations in taking on the common threats of the 21st century - terrorism and climate change; genocide and disease?

Can we send a message to all those weary travelers beyond our shores who long to be free from fear and want that the United States of America is, and always will be, 'the last best, hope of Earth?

We say; we hope; we believe - yes we can.

A More Perfect Union
"The Race Speech"
Philadelphia, PA
March 18, 2008

"We the people, in order to form a more perfect union."

Two hundred and twenty one years ago, in a hall that still stands across the street, a group of men gathered and, with these simple words, launched America's improbable experiment in democracy. Farmers and scholars; statesmen and patriots who had traveled across an ocean to escape tyranny and persecution finally made real their declaration of independence at a Philadelphia convention that lasted through the spring of 1787.

The document they produced was eventually signed but ultimately unfinished. It was stained by this nation's original sin of slavery, a question that divided the colonies and brought the convention to a stalemate until the founders chose to allow the slave trade to continue for at least twenty more years, and to leave any final resolution to future generations.

Of course, the answer to the slavery question was already embedded within our Constitution - a Constitution that had at is very core the ideal of equal citizenship under the law; a Constitution that promised its people liberty, and justice, and a union that could be and should be perfected over time.

And yet words on a parchment would not be enough to deliver slaves from bondage, or provide men and women of every color and creed their full rights and obligations as citizens of the United States. What would be needed were Americans in successive generations who were willing to do their part - through protests and struggle, on the streets and in the courts, through a civil war and civil disobedience and always at great risk - to narrow that gap between the promise of our ideals and the reality of their time.

This was one of the tasks we set forth at the beginning of this campaign - to continue the long march of those who came before us, a march for a more just, more equal, more free, more caring and more prosperous America. I chose to run for the presidency at this moment in history because I believe deeply that we cannot solve the challenges of our time unless we solve them together - unless we perfect our union by understanding that we may have different stories, but we hold common hopes; that we may not look the same and we may not have come from the same place, but we all want to move in the same direction - towards a better future for our children and our grandchildren.

This belief comes from my unyielding faith in the decency and generosity of the American people. But it also comes from my own American story.

I am the son of a black man from Kenya and a white woman from Kansas. I was raised with the help of a white grandfather who survived a Depression to serve in Patton's Army during World War II and a white grandmother who worked on a bomber assembly line at Fort Leavenworth while he was overseas. I've gone to some of the best schools in America and lived in one of the world's poorest nations. I am married to a black American who carries within her the blood of slaves and slaveowners - an inheritance we pass on to our two precious daughters. I have brothers, sisters, nieces, nephews, uncles and cousins, of every race and every hue, scattered across three continents, and for as long as I live, I will never forget that in no other country on Earth is my story even possible.

It's a story that hasn't made me the most conventional candidate. But it is a story that has seared into my genetic makeup the idea that this nation is more than the sum of its parts - that out of many, we are truly one.

Throughout the first year of this campaign, against all predictions to the contrary, we saw how hungry the American people were for this message of unity. Despite the temptation to view my candidacy through a purely racial lens, we won commanding victories in states with some of the whitest populations in the country. In South Carolina, where the Confederate Flag still flies, we built a powerful coalition of African Americans and white Americans.

This is not to say that race has not been an issue in the campaign. At various stages in the campaign, some commentators have deemed me either "too black" or "not black enough." We saw racial tensions bubble to the surface during the week before the South Carolina primary. The press has scoured every exit poll for the latest evidence of racial polarization, not just in terms of white and black, but black and brown as well.

And yet, it has only been in the last couple of weeks that the discussion of race in this campaign has taken a particularly divisive turn.

On one end of the spectrum, we've heard the implication that my candidacy is somehow an exercise in affirmative action; that it's based solely on the desire of wide-eyed liberals to purchase racial reconciliation on the cheap. On the other end, we've heard my former pastor, Reverend Jeremiah Wright, use incendiary language to express views that have the potential not only to widen the racial divide, but views that denigrate both the greatness and the goodness of our nation; that rightly offend white and black alike.

I have already condemned, in unequivocal terms, the statements of Reverend Wright that have caused such controversy. For some, nagging questions remain. Did I know him to be an occasionally fierce critic of American domestic and foreign policy? Of course. Did I ever hear him make remarks that could be considered controversial while I sat in church? Yes. Did I strongly disagree with many of his political views? Absolutely - just as I'm sure many of you have heard remarks from your pastors, priests, or rabbis with which you strongly disagreed.

But the remarks that have caused this recent firestorm weren't simply controversial. They weren't simply a religious leader's effort to speak out against perceived injustice. Instead, they expressed a profoundly distorted view of this country - a view that sees white racism as endemic, and that elevates what is wrong with America above all that we know is right with America; a view that sees the conflicts in the Middle East as rooted primarily in the actions of stalwart allies like Israel, instead of emanating from the perverse and hateful ideologies of radical Islam.

As such, Reverend Wright's comments were not only wrong but divisive, divisive at a time when we need unity; racially charged at a time when we need to come together to solve a set of monumental problems - two wars, a terrorist threat, a falling economy, a chronic health care crisis and potentially devastating climate change; problems that are neither black or white or Latino or Asian, but rather problems that confront us all.

Given my background, my politics, and my professed values and ideals, there will no doubt be those for whom my statements of condemnation are not enough. Why associate myself with Reverend Wright in the first place, they may ask? Why not join another church? And I confess that if all that I knew of Reverend Wright were the snippets of those sermons that have run in an endless loop on the television and You Tube, or if Trinity United Church of Christ conformed to the caricatures being peddled by some commentators, there is no doubt that I would react in much the same way

But the truth is, that isn't all that I know of the man. The man I met more than twenty years ago is a man who helped introduce me to my Christian faith, a man who spoke to me about our obligations to love one another; to care for the sick and lift up the poor. He is a man who served his country as a U.S. Marine; who has studied and lectured at some of the finest universities and seminaries in the country, and who for over thirty years led a church that serves the community by doing God's work here on Earth - by housing the homeless, ministering to the needy, providing day care services and scholarships and prison ministries, and reaching out to those suffering from HIV/AIDS.

In my first book, Dreams From My Father, I described the experience of my first service at Trinity:

"People began to shout, to rise from their seats and clap and cry out, a forceful wind carrying the reverend's voice up into the rafters....And in that single note - hope! - I heard something else; at the foot of that cross, inside the thousands of churches across the city, I imagined the stories of ordinary black people merging with the stories of David and Goliath, Moses and Pharaoh, the Christians in the lion's den, Ezekiel's field of dry bones. Those stories - of survival, and freedom, and hope - became our story, my story; the blood that had spilled was our blood, the tears our tears; until this black church, on this bright day, seemed once more a vessel carrying the story of a people into future generations and into a larger world. Our trials and triumphs became at once unique and universal, black and more than black; in chronicling our journey, the stories and songs gave us a means to reclaim memories that we didn't need to feel shame about...memories that all people might study and cherish - and with which we could start to rebuild."

That has been my experience at Trinity. Like other

predominantly black churches across the country, Trinity embodies the black community in its entirety - the doctor and the welfare mom, the model student and the former gang-banger. Like other black churches, Trinity's services are full of raucous laughter and sometimes bawdy humor. They are full of dancing, clapping, screaming and shouting that may seem jarring to the untrained ear. The church contains in full the kindness and cruelty, the fierce intelligence and the shocking ignorance, the struggles and successes, the love and yes, the bitterness and bias that make up the black experience in America.

And this helps explain, perhaps, my relationship with Reverend Wright. As imperfect as he may be, he has been like family to me. He strengthened my faith, officiated my wedding, and baptized my children. Not once in my conversations with him have I heard him talk about any ethnic group in derogatory terms, or treat whites with whom he interacted with anything but courtesy and respect. He contains within him the contradictions - the good and the bad - of the community that he has served diligently for so many years.

I can no more disown him than I can disown the black community. I can no more disown him than I can my white grandmother - a woman who helped raise me, a woman who sacrificed again and again for me, a woman who loves me as much as she loves anything in this world, but a woman who once confessed her fear of black men who passed by her on the street, and who on more than one occasion has uttered racial or ethnic stereotypes that made me cringe.

These people are a part of me. And they are a part of America, this country that I love.

Some will see this as an attempt to justify or excuse comments that are simply inexcusable. I can assure you it is not. I suppose the politically safe thing would be to move on from this episode and just hope that it fades into the woodwork. We can dismiss Reverend Wright as a crank or a demagogue, just as some have dismissed Geraldine Ferraro, in the aftermath of her recent statements, as harboring some deep-seated racial bias.

But race is an issue that I believe this nation cannot afford to ignore right now. We would be making the same mistake that Reverend Wright made in his offending sermons about America - to simplify and stereotype and amplify the negative to the point that it distorts reality.

The fact is that the comments that have been made and the issues that have surfaced over the last few weeks reflect the complexities of race in this country that we've never really worked through - a part of our union that we have yet to perfect. And if we walk away now, if we simply retreat into our respective corners, we will never be able to come together and solve challenges like health care, or education, or the need to find good jobs for every American.

Understanding this reality requires a reminder of how we arrived at this point. As William Faulkner once wrote, "The past isn't dead and buried. In fact, it isn't even past." We do not need to recite here the history of racial injustice in this country. But we do need to remind ourselves that so many of the disparities that exist in the African-American community today can be directly traced to inequalities passed on from an earlier generation that suffered under the brutal legacy of slavery and Jim Crow.

Segregated schools were, and are, inferior schools; we still haven't fixed them, fifty years after Brown v. Board of Education, and the inferior education they provided, then and now, helps explain the pervasive achievement gap between today's black and white students.

Legalized discrimination - where blacks were prevented, often through violence, from owning property, or loans were not granted to African-American business owners, or black homeowners could not access FHA mortgages, or blacks were excluded from unions, or the police force, or fire departments - meant that black families could not amass any meaningful wealth to bequeath to future generations. That history helps explain the wealth and income gap between black and white, and the concentrated pockets of poverty that persists in so many of today's urban and rural communities.

A lack of economic opportunity among black men, and the shame and frustration that came from not being able to provide for one's family, contributed to the erosion of black families - a problem that welfare policies for many years may have worsened. And the lack of basic services in so many urban black neighborhoods - parks for kids to play in, police walking the beat, regular garbage pick-up and building code enforcement - all helped create a cycle of violence, blight and neglect that continue to haunt us.

This is the reality in which Reverend Wright and other African-Americans of his generation grew up. They came of age in the late fifties and early sixties, a time when segregation was still the law of the land and opportunity was systematically constricted. What's remarkable is not how many failed in the face of discrimination, but rather how many men and women overcame the odds; how many were able to make a way out of no way for those like me who would come after them.

But for all those who scratched and clawed their way to get a piece of the American Dream, there were many who didn't make it - those who were ultimately defeated, in one way or another, by discrimination. That legacy of defeat was passed on to future generations - those young men and increasingly young women who we see standing on street corners or languishing in our prisons, without hope or prospects for the future. Even for those blacks who did make it, questions of race, and racism, continue to define their worldview in fundamental ways. For the men and women of Reverend Wright's generation, the memories of humiliation and doubt and fear have not gone away; nor has the anger and the bitterness of those years. That anger may not get expressed in public, in front of white co-workers or white friends. But it does find voice in the barbershop or around the kitchen table. At times, that anger is exploited by politicians, to gin up votes along racial lines, or to make up for a politician's own failings.

And occasionally it finds voice in the church on Sunday

morning, in the pulpit and in the pews. The fact that so many people are surprised to hear that anger in some of Reverend Wright's sermons simply reminds us of the old truism that the most segregated hour in American life occurs on Sunday morning. That anger is not always productive; indeed, all too often it distracts attention from solving real problems; it keeps us from squarely facing our own complicity in our condition, and prevents the African-American community from forging the alliances it needs to bring about real change. But the anger is real; it is powerful; and to simply wish it away, to condemn it without understanding its roots, only serves to widen the chasm of misunderstanding that exists between the races.

In fact, a similar anger exists within segments of the white community. Most working- and middle-class white Americans don't feel that they have been particularly privileged by their race. Their experience is the immigrant experience - as far as they're concerned, no one's handed them anything, they've built it from scratch. They've worked hard all their lives, many times only to see their jobs shipped overseas or their pension dumped after a lifetime of labor. They are anxious about their futures, and feel their dreams slipping away; in an era of stagnant wages and global competition, opportunity comes to be seen as a zero sum game, in which your dreams come at my expense. So when they are told to bus their children to a school across town; when they hear that an African American is getting an advantage in landing a good job or a spot in a good college because of an injustice that they themselves never committed; when they're told that their fears about crime in urban neighborhoods are somehow prejudiced, resentment builds over time.

Like the anger within the black community, these resentments aren't always expressed in polite company. But they have helped shape the political landscape for at least a generation. Anger over welfare and affirmative action helped forge the Reagan Coalition. Politicians routinely exploited fears of crime for their own electoral ends. Talk show hosts and conservative commentators built entire careers unmasking bogus claims of racism while dismissing legitimate discussions of racial injustice and inequality as mere political correctness or reverse racism.

Just as black anger often proved counterproductive, so have these white resentments distracted attention from the real culprits of the middle class squeeze - a corporate culture rife with inside dealing, questionable accounting practices, and short-term greed; a Washington dominated by lobbyists and special interests; economic policies that favor the few over the many. And yet, to wish away the resentments of white Americans, to label them as misguided or even racist, without recognizing they are grounded in legitimate concerns - this too widens the racial divide, and blocks the path to understanding.

This is where we are right now. It's a racial stalemate we've been stuck in for years. Contrary to the claims of some of my critics, black and white, I have never been so naïve as to believe that we can get beyond our racial divisions in a single election cycle, or with a single candidacy - particularly a candidacy as imperfect as my own.

But I have asserted a firm conviction - a conviction rooted in my faith in God and my faith in the American people - that working together we can move beyond some of our old racial wounds, and that in fact we have no choice if we are to continue on the path of a more perfect union.

For the African-American community, that path means embracing the burdens of our past without becoming victims of our past. It means continuing to insist on a full measure of justice in every aspect of American life. But it also means binding our particular grievances - for better health care, and better schools, and better jobs - to the larger aspirations of all Americans -- the white woman struggling to break the glass ceiling, the white man whose been laid off, the immigrant trying to feed his family. And it means taking full responsibility for own lives - by demanding more from our fathers, and spending more time with our children, and reading to them, and teaching them that while they may face challenges and discrimination in their own lives, they must never succumb to despair or cynicism; they must always believe that they can write their own destiny.

Ironically, this quintessentially American - and yes, conservative - notion of self-help found frequent expression in Reverend Wright's sermons. But what my former pastor too often failed to understand is that embarking on a program of self-help also requires a belief that society can change.

The profound mistake of Reverend Wright's sermons is not that he spoke about racism in our society. It's that he spoke as if our society was static; as if no progress has been made; as if this country - a country that has made it possible for one of his own members to run for the highest office in the land and build a coalition of white and black; Latino and Asian, rich and poor, young and old -- is still irrevocably bound to a tragic past. But what we know -- what we have seen - is that America can change. That is true genius of this nation. What we have already achieved gives us hope - the audacity to hope - for what we can and must achieve tomorrow.

In the white community, the path to a more perfect union means acknowledging that what ails the African-American community does not just exist in the minds of black people; that the legacy of discrimination - and current incidents of discrimination, while less overt than in the past - are real and must be addressed. Not just with words, but with deeds - by investing in our schools and our communities; by enforcing our civil rights laws and ensuring fairness in our criminal justice system; by providing this generation with ladders of opportunity that were unavailable for previous generations. It requires all Americans to realize that your dreams do not have to come at the expense of my dreams; that investing in the health, welfare, and education of black and brown and white children will ultimately help all of America prosper.

In the end, then, what is called for is nothing more, and nothing less, than what all the world's great religions demand - that we do unto others as we would have them do unto us. Let us be our brother's keeper, Scripture tells us. Let us be our sister's keeper. Let us find that common stake we all have in one another, and let our politics reflect that spirit as well.

For we have a choice in this country. We can accept a politics that breeds division, and conflict, and cynicism. We can tackle race only as spectacle - as we did in the OJ trial - or in the wake of tragedy, as we did in the aftermath of Katrina - or as fodder for the nightly news. We can play Reverend Wright's sermons on every channel, every day and talk about them from now until the election, and make the only question in this campaign whether or not the American people think that I somehow believe or sympathize with his most offensive words. We can pounce on some gaffe by a Hillary supporter as evidence that she's playing the race card, or we can speculate on whether white men will all flock to John McCain in the general election regardless of his policies.

We can do that.

But if we do, I can tell you that in the next election, we'll be talking about some other distraction. And then another one. And then another one. And nothing will change.

That is one option. Or, at this moment, in this election, we can come together and say, "Not this time." This time we want to talk about the crumbling schools that are stealing the future of black children and white children and Asian children and Hispanic children and Native American children. This time we want to reject the cynicism that tells us that these kids can't learn; that those kids who don't look like us are somebody else's problem. The children of America are not those kids, they are our kids, and we will not let them fall behind in a 21st century economy. Not this time.

This time we want to talk about how the lines in the Emergency Room are filled with whites and blacks and Hispanics who do not have health care; who don't have the power on their own to overcome the special interests in Washington, but who can take them on if we do it together.

This time we want to talk about the shuttered mills that once provided a decent life for men and women of every race, and the homes for sale that once belonged to Americans from every religion, every region, every walk of life. This time we want to talk about the fact that the real problem is not that someone who doesn't look like you might take your job; it's that the corporation you work for will ship it overseas for nothing more than a profit.

This time we want to talk about the men and women of every color and creed who serve together, and fight together, and bleed together under the same proud flag. We want to talk about how to bring them home from a war that never should've been authorized and never should've been waged, and we want to talk about how we'll show our patriotism by caring for them, and their families, and giving them the benefits they have earned.

I would not be running for President if I didn't believe with all my heart that this is what the vast majority of Americans want for this country. This union may never be perfect, but generation after generation has shown that it can always be perfected. And today, whenever I find myself feeling doubtful or cynical about this possibility, what gives me the most hope is the next generation - the young people whose attitudes and beliefs and openness to change have already made history in this election.

There is one story in particularly that I'd like to leave you with today - a story I told when I had the great honor of speaking on Dr. King's birthday at his home church, Ebenezer Baptist, in Atlanta.

There is a young, twenty-three year old white woman named Ashley Baia who organized for our campaign in Florence, South Carolina. She had been working to organize a mostly African-American community since the beginning of this campaign, and one day she was at a roundtable discussion where everyone went around telling their story and why they were there.

And Ashley said that when she was nine years old, her mother got cancer. And because she had to miss days of work, she was let go and lost her health care. They had to file for bankruptcy, and that's when Ashley decided that she had to do something to help her mom.

She knew that food was one of their most expensive costs, and so Ashley convinced her mother that what she really liked and really wanted to eat more than anything else was mustard and relish sandwiches. Because that was the cheapest way to eat.

She did this for a year until her mom got better, and she told everyone at the roundtable that the reason she joined our campaign was so that she could help the millions of other children in the country who want and need to help their parents too.

Now Ashley might have made a different choice. Perhaps somebody told her along the way that the source of her mother's problems were blacks who were on welfare and too lazy to work, or Hispanics who were coming into the country illegally. But she didn't. She sought out allies in her fight against injustice.

Anyway, Ashley finishes her story and then goes around the room and asks everyone else why they're supporting the campaign. They all have different stories and reasons. Many bring up a specific issue. And finally they come to this elderly black man who's been sitting there quietly the entire time. And Ashley asks him why he's there. And he does not bring up a specific issue. He does not say health care or the economy. He does not say education or the war. He does not say that he was there because of Barack Obama. He simply says to everyone in the room, "I am here because of Ashley."

"I'm here because of Ashley." By itself, that single moment of recognition between that young white girl and that old black man is not enough. It is not enough to give health care to the sick, or jobs to the jobless, or education to our children.

But it is where we start. It is where our union grows stronger. And as so many generations have come to realize over the course of the two-hundred and twenty one years since a band of patriots signed that document in Philadelphia, that is where the perfection begins.

AP Annual Luncheon
Washington, DC
April 14, 2008

> *Editor's note: The week before this speech,*
> *Obama was caught in an uncharacteristic*
> *moment of loose language. Referring to*
> *working-class voters in old industrial towns*
> *impacted by job losses, the presidential hopeful*
> *said: "They get bitter, they cling to guns or*
> *religion or antipathy to people who aren't like*
> *them or anti-immigrant sentiment or*
> *anti-trade sentiment, as a way to explain their*
> *frustrations."*

Good afternoon. I know I kept a lot of you guys busy this weekend with the comments I made last week. Some of you might even be a little bitter about that.

As I said yesterday, I regret some of the words I chose, partly because the way that these remarks have been interpreted have offended some people and partly because they have served as one more distraction from the critical debate that we must have in this election season.

I'm a person of deep faith, and my religion has sustained me through a lot in my life. I even gave a speech on faith before I ever started running for President where I said that Democrats, "make a mistake when we fail to acknowledge the power of faith in people's lives." I also represent a state with a large number of hunters and sportsmen, and I understand how important these traditions are to families in Illinois and all across America. And, contrary to what my poor word choices may have implied or my opponents have suggested, I've never believed that these traditions or people's faith has anything to do with how much money they have.

But I will never walk away from the larger point that I was trying to make. For the last several decades, people in small towns and cities and rural areas all across this country have seen globalization change the rules of the game on them. When I began my career as an organizer on the South Side of Chicago, I saw what happens when the local steel mill shuts its doors and moves overseas. You don't just lose the jobs in the mill, you start losing jobs and businesses throughout the community. The streets are emptier. The schools suffer.

I saw it during my campaign for the Senate in Illinois when I'd talk to union guys who had worked at the local Maytag plant for twenty, thirty years before being laid off at fifty-five years old when it picked up and moved to Mexico; and they had no idea what they're going to do without the paycheck or the pension that they counted on. One man didn't even know if he'd be able to afford the liver transplant his son needed now that his health care was gone.

I've heard these stories almost every day during this campaign, whether it was in Iowa or Ohio or Pennsylvania. And the people I've met have also told me that every year, in every election, politicians come to their towns, and they tell them what they want to hear, and they make big promises, and then they go back to Washington when the campaign's over, and nothing changes. There's no plan to address the downside of globalization. We don't do anything about the skyrocketing cost of health care or college or those disappearing pensions. Instead of fighting to replace jobs that aren't coming back, Washington ends up fighting over the latest distraction of the week.

And after years and years and years of this, a lot of people in this country have become cynical about what government can do to improve their lives. They are angry and frustrated with their leaders for not listening to them; for not fighting for them; for not always telling them the truth. And yes, they are bitter about that.

Now, Senator McCain and the Republicans in Washington are already looking ahead to the fall and have decided that they plan on using these comments to argue that I'm out of touch with what's going on in the lives of working Americans. I don't blame them for this -- that's the nature of our political culture, and if I had to carry the banner for eight years of George Bush's failures, I'd be looking for something else to talk about too.

But I will say this. If John McCain wants to turn this election into a contest about which party is out of touch with the struggles and the hopes of working America, that's a debate I'm happy to have. In fact, I think that's a debate we need to have. Because I believe that the real insult to the millions of hard-working Americans out there would be a continuation of the economic agenda that has dominated Washington for far too long.

I may have made a mistake last week in the words that I chose, but the other party has made a much more damaging mistake in the failed policies they've chosen and the bankrupt philosophy they've embraced for the last three decades.

It's a philosophy that says there's no role for government in making the global economy work for working Americas; that we have to just sit back watch those factories close and those jobs disappear; that there's nothing we can do or should do about workers without health care, or children in crumbling schools, or families who are losing their homes, and so we should just hand out a few tax breaks and wish everyone the best of luck.

Ronald Reagan called this trickle-down economics. George Bush called it the Ownership Society. But what it really means is that you're on your own. If your premiums or your tuition is rising faster than you can afford, you're on your own. If you're that Maytag worker who just lost his pension, tough luck. If you're a child born into poverty, you'll just have to pull yourself up by your own bootstraps.

This philosophy isn't just out-of-touch - it's put our economy out-of-whack. Years of pain on Main Street have finally trickled up to Wall Street and sent us hurtling toward recession, reminding us that we're all connected - that we can't prosper as a nation where a few people are doing well and everyone else is struggling.

John McCain is an American hero and a worthy opponent, but he's proven time and time again that he just doesn't understand this. It took him three tries in seven days just to figure out that the home foreclosure crisis was an actual problem. He's had a front row seat to the last eight years of disastrous policies that have widened the income gap and saddled our children with debt, and now he's promising four more years of the very same thing.

He's promising to make permanent the Bush tax breaks for the wealthiest few who didn't need them and didn't ask for them - tax breaks that are so irresponsible that John McCain himself once said they offended his conscience.

He's promising four more years of trade deals that don't have a single safeguard for American workers - that don't help American workers compete and win in a global economy.

He's promising four more years of an Administration that will push for the privatization of Social Security - a plan that would gamble away people's retirement on the stock market; a plan that was already rejected by Democrats and Republicans under George Bush.

He's promising four more years of policies that won't guarantee health insurance for working Americans; that won't bring down the rising cost of college tuition; that won't do a thing for the Americans who are living in those communities where the jobs have left and the factories have shut their doors.

And yet, despite all this, the other side is still betting that the American people won't notice that John McCain is running for George Bush's third term. They think that they'll forget about all that's happened in the last eight years; that they'll be tricked into believing that it's either me or our party is the one that's out of touch with what's going on in their lives.

Well I'm making a different bet. I'm betting on the American people.

The men and women I've met in small towns and big cities across this country see this election as a defining moment in our history. They understand what's at stake here because they're living it every day. And they are tired of being distracted by fake controversies. They are fed up with politicians trying to divide us for their own political gain. And I believe they'll see through the tactics that are used every year, in every election, to appeal to our fears, or our biases, or our differences - because they've never wanted or needed change as badly as they do now.

The people I've met during this campaign know that government cannot solve all of our problems, and they don't expect it to. They don't want our tax dollars wasted on programs that don't work or perks for special interests who don't work for us. They understand that we cannot stop every job from going overseas or build a wall around our economy, and they know that we shouldn't.

But they believe it's finally time that we make health care affordable and available for every single American; that we bring down costs for workers and for businesses; that we cut premiums, and stop insurance companies from denying people care or coverage who need it most.

They believe it's time we provided real relief to the victims of this housing crisis; that we help families refinance their mortgage so they can stay in their homes; that we start giving tax relief to the people who actually need it - middle-class families, and seniors, and struggling homeowners.

They believe that we can and should make the global economy work for working Americans; that we might not be able to stop every job from going overseas, but we certainly can stop giving tax breaks to companies who send them their and start giving tax breaks to companies who create good jobs right here in America. We can invest in the types of renewable energy that won't just reduce our dependence on oil and save our planet, but create up to five million new jobs that can't be outsourced.

They believe we can train our workers for those new jobs, and keep the most productive workforce the most competitive workforce in the world if we fix our public education system by investing in what works and finding out what doesn't; if we invest in early childhood education and finally make college affordable for everyone who wants to go; if we stop talking about how great our teachers are and start rewarding them for their greatness.

They believe that if you work your entire life, you deserve to retire with dignity and respect, which means a pension you can count on, and Social Security that's always there.

This is what the people I've met believe about the country they love. It doesn't matter if they're Democrats or Republicans; whether they're from the smallest towns or the biggest cities; whether they hunt or they don't; whether they go to church, or temple, or mosque, or not. We may come from different places and have different stories, but we share common hopes, and one very American dream.

That is the dream I am running to help restore in this election. If I get the chance, that is what I'll be talking about from now until November. That is the choice that I'll offer the American people - four more years of what we had for the last eight, or fundamental change in Washington.

People may be bitter about their leaders and the state of our politics, but beneath that, they are hopeful about what's possible in America. That's why they leave their homes on their day off, or their jobs after a long day of work, and travel - sometimes for miles, sometimes in the bitter cold - to attend a rally or a town hall meeting held by Senator Clinton, or Senator McCain, or myself. Because they believe that we can change things. Because they believe in that dream.

I know something about that dream. I wasn't born into a lot of money. I was raised by a single mother with the help my grandparents, who grew up in small-town Kansas, went to school on the GI Bill, and bought their home through an FHA loan. My mother had to use food stamps at one point, but she still made sure that through scholarships, I got a chance to go to some of the best schools around, which helped me get into some of the best colleges around, which gave me loans that Michelle and I just finished paying not all that many years ago.

In other words, my story is a quintessentially American story. It's the same story that has made this country a beacon for the world-a story of struggle and sacrifice on the part of my forebearers and a story overcoming great odds. I carry that story with me each and every day, It's why I wake up every day and do this, and it's why I continue to hold such hope for the future of a country where the dreams of its people have always been possible. Thank you.

Pennsylvania Primary Night
Evansville, Indiana
April 22, 2008

I want to start by congratulating Senator Clinton on her victory tonight, and I want to thank the hundreds of thousands of Pennsylvanians who stood with our campaign today.

There were a lot of folks who didn't think we could make this a close race when it started. But we worked hard, and we traveled across the state to big cities and small towns, to factory floors and VFW halls. And now, six weeks later, we closed the gap. We rallied people of every age and race and background to our cause. And whether they were inspired for the first time or for the first time in a long time, we registered a record number of voters who will lead our party to victory in November.

These Americans cast their ballot for the same reason you came here tonight; for the same reason that millions of Americans have gone door-to-door and given whatever small amount they can to this campaign; for the same reason that we began this journey just a few hundred miles from here on a cold February morning in Springfield - because we believe that the challenges we face are bigger than the smallness of our politics, and we know that this election is our chance to change it.

After fourteen long months, it's easy to forget this from time to time - to lose sight of the fierce urgency of this moment. It's easy to get caught up in the distractions and the silliness and the tit-for-tat that consumes our politics; the bickering that none of us are immune to, and that trivializes the profound issues - two wars, an economy in recession, a planet in peril.

But that kind of politics is not why we're here. It's not why I'm here and it's not why you're here.

We're here because of the more than one hundred workers in Logansport, Indiana who just found out that their company has decided to move its entire factory to Taiwan.

We're here because of the young man I met in Youngsville, North Carolina who almost lost his home because he has three children with cystic fibrosis and couldn't pay their medical bills; who still doesn't have health insurance for himself or his wife and lives in fear that a single illness could cost them everything.

We're here because there are families all across this country who are sitting around the kitchen table right now trying to figure out how to pay their insurance premiums, and their kids' tuition, and still make the mortgage so they're not the next ones in the neighborhood to put a For Sale sign in the front yard; who will lay awake tonight wondering if next week's paycheck will cover next month's bills.

We're not here to talk about change for change's sake, but because our families, our communities, and our country desperately need it. We're here because we can't afford to keep doing what we've been doing for another four years. We can't afford to play the same Washington games with the same Washington players and expect a different result. Not this time. Not now.

We already know what we're getting from the other party's nominee. John McCain has offered this country a lifetime of service, and we respect that, but what he's not offering is any meaningful change from the policies of George W. Bush.

John McCain believes that George Bush's Iraq policy is a success, so he's offering four more years of a war with no exit strategy; a war that's sending our troops on their third tour, and fourth tour, and fifth tour of duty; a war that's costing us billions of dollars a month and hasn't made us any safer.

John McCain said that George Bush's economic policies have led to "great progress" over the last seven years, and so he's promising four more years of tax cuts for CEOs and corporations who didn't need them and weren't asking for them; tax cuts that he once voted against because he said they "offended his conscience."

Well they may have stopped offending John McCain's conscience somewhere along the road to the White House, but George Bush's economic policies still offend ours. Because I don't think that the 232,000 Americans who've lost their jobs this year are seeing the great progress that John McCain has seen. I don't think the millions of Americans losing their homes have seen that progress. I don't think the families without health care and the workers without pensions have seen that progress. And if we continue down the same reckless path, I don't think that future generations who'll be saddled with debt will see these as years of progress.

We already know that John McCain offers more of the same.

The question is not whether the other party will bring about change in Washington - the question is, will we?

Because the truth is, the challenges we face are not just the fault of one man or one party. How many years - how many decades - have we been talking about solving our health care crisis? How many Presidents have promised to end our dependence on foreign oil? How many jobs have gone overseas in the 70s, and the 80s, and the 90s? And we still haven't done anything about it. And we know why.

In every election, politicians come to your cities and your towns, and they tell you what you want to hear, and they make big promises, and they lay out all these plans and policies. But then they go back to Washington when the campaign's over. Lobbyists spend millions of dollars to get their way. The status quo sets in. And instead of fighting for health care or jobs, Washington ends up fighting over the latest distraction of the week. It happens year after year after year.

Well this is your chance to say "Not this year." This is your chance to say "Not this time." We have a choice in this election.

We can be a party that says there's no problem with taking money from Washington lobbyists - from oil lobbyists and drug lobbyists and insurance lobbyists. We can pretend that they represent real Americans and look the other way when they use their money and influence to stop us from reforming health care or investing in renewable energy for yet another four years.

Or this time, we can recognize that you can't be the champion of working Americans if you're funded by the lobbyists who drown out their voices. We can do what we've done in this campaign, and say that we won't take a dime of their money. We can do what I did in Illinois, and in Washington, and bring both parties together to rein in their power so we can take our government back. It's our choice.

We can be a party that thinks the only way to look tough on national security is to talk, and act, and vote like George Bush and John McCain. We can use fear as a tactic, and the threat of terrorism to scare up votes.

Or we can decide that real strength is asking the tough questions before we send our troops to fight. We can see the threats we face for what they are - a call to rally all Americans and all the world against the common challenges of the 21st century - terrorism and nuclear weapons; climate change and poverty; genocide and disease. That's what it takes to keep us safe in the world. That's the real legacy of Roosevelt and Kennedy and Truman.

We can be a party that says and does whatever it takes to win the next election. We can calculate and poll-test our positions and tell everyone exactly what they want to hear.

Or we can be the party that doesn't just focus on how to win but why we should. We can tell everyone what they need to hear about the challenges we face. We can seek to regain not just an office, but the trust of the American people that their leaders in Washington will tell them the truth. That's the choice in this election.

We can be a party of those who only think like we do and only agree with all our positions. We can continue to slice and dice this country into Red States and Blue States. We can exploit the divisions that exist in our country for pure political gain.

Or this time, we can build on the movement we've started in this campaign - a movement that's united Democrats, Independents, and Republicans; a movement of young and old, rich and poor; white, black, Hispanic, Asian, and Native American. Because one thing I know from traveling to forty-six states this campaign season is that we're not as divided as our politics suggests. We may have different stories and different backgrounds, but we hold common hopes for the future of this country.

In the end, this election is still our best chance to solve the problems we've been talking about for decades - as one nation; as one people. Fourteen months later, that is still what this election is about.

Millions of Americans who believe we can do better - that we must do better - have put us in a position to bring about real change. Now it's up to you, Indiana. You can decide whether we're going to travel the same worn path, or whether we chart a new course that offers real hope for the future.

During the course of this campaign, we've all learned what my wife reminds me of all the time - that I am not a perfect man. And I will not be a perfect President. And so while I will always listen to you, and be honest with you, and fight for you every single day for the next for years, I will also ask you to be a part of the change that we need. Because in my two decades of public service to this country, I have seen time and time again that real change doesn't begin in the halls of Washington, but on the streets of America. It doesn't happen from the top-down, it happens from the bottom-up.

I also know that real change has never been easy, and it won't be easy this time either. The status quo in Washington will fight harder than they ever have to divide us and distract us with ads and attacks from now until November.

But don't ever forget that you have the power to change this country.

You can make this election about how we're going to help those workers in Logansport; how we're going to re-train them, and educate them, and make our workforce competitive in a global economy.

You can make this election about how we're going to make health care affordable for that family in North Carolina; how we're going to help those families sitting around the kitchen table tonight pay their bills and stay in their homes.

You can make this election about how we plan to leave our children and all children a planet that's safer and a world that still sees America the same way my father saw it from across the ocean - as a beacon of all that is good and all that is possible for all mankind.

It is now our turn to follow in the footsteps of all those generations who sacrificed and struggled and faced down the greatest odds to perfect our improbable union. And if we're willing to do what they did; if we're willing to shed our cynicism and our doubts and our fears; if we're willing to believe in what's possible again; then I believe that we won't just win this primary election, we won't just win this election in November, we will change this country, and keep this country's promise alive in the twenty-first century. Thank you, and may God Bless the United States of America.

Primary Night: North Carolina
Raleigh, NC
May 6, 2008

You know, some were saying that North Carolina would be a game-changer in this election. But today, what North Carolina decided is that the only game that needs changing is the one in Washington, DC.

I want to start by congratulating Senator Clinton on her victory in the state of Indiana. And I want to thank the people of North Carolina for giving us a victory in a big state, a swing state, and a state where we will compete to win if I am the Democratic nominee for President of the United States.

When this campaign began, Washington didn't give us much of a chance. But because you came out in the bitter cold, and knocked on doors, and enlisted your friends and neighbors in this cause; because you stood up to the cynics, and the doubters, and the nay-sayers when we were up and when we were down; because you still believe that this is our moment, and our time, for change – tonight we stand less than two hundred delegates away from securing the Democratic nomination for President of the United States.

More importantly, because of you, we have seen that it's possible to overcome the politics of division and distraction; that it's possible to overcome the same old negative attacks that are always about scoring points and never about solving our problems. We've seen that the American people aren't looking for more spin or more gimmicks, but honest answers about the challenges we face. That's what you've accomplished in this campaign, and that's how we'll change this country together.

This has been one of the longest, most closely fought contests in history. And that's partly because we have such a formidable opponent in Senator Hillary Clinton. Tonight, many of the pundits have suggested that this party is inalterably divided – that Senator Clinton's supporters will not support me, and that my supporters will not support her.

Well I'm here tonight to tell you that I don't believe it. Yes, there have been bruised feelings on both sides. Yes, each side desperately wants their candidate to win. But ultimately, this race is not about Hillary Clinton or Barack Obama or John McCain. This election is about you – the American people – and whether we will have a president and a party that can lead us toward a brighter future.

This primary season may not be over, but when it is, we will have to remember who we are as Democrats – that we are the party of Jefferson and Jackson; of Roosevelt and Kennedy; and that we are at our best when we lead with principle; when we lead with conviction; when we summon an entire nation around a common purpose – a higher purpose. This fall, we intend to march forward as one Democratic Party, united by a common vision for this country. Because we all agree that at this defining moment in history – a moment when we're facing two wars, an economy in turmoil, a planet in peril – we can't afford to give John McCain the chance to serve out

George Bush's third term. We need change in America.

The woman I met in Indiana who just lost her job, and her pension, and her insurance when the plant where she worked at her entire life closed down – she can't afford four more years of tax breaks for corporations like the one that shipped her job overseas. She needs us to give tax breaks to companies that create good jobs here in America. She can't afford four more years of tax breaks for CEOs like the one who walked away from her company with a multi-million dollar bonus. She needs middle-class tax relief that will help her pay the skyrocketing price of groceries, and gas, and college tuition. That's why I'm running for President.

The college student I met in Iowa who works the night shift after a full day of class and still can't pay the medical bills for a sister who's ill – she can't afford four more years of a health care plan that only takes care of the healthy and the wealthy; that allows insurance companies to discriminate and deny coverage to those Americans who need it most. She needs us to stand up to those insurance companies and pass a plan that lowers every family's premiums and gives every uninsured American the same kind of coverage that Members of Congress give themselves. That's why I'm running for President.

The mother in Wisconsin who gave me a bracelet inscribed with the name of the son she lost in Iraq; the families who pray for their loved ones to come home; the heroes on their third and fourth and fifth tour of duty – they can't afford four more years of a war that should've never been authorized and never been waged. They can't afford four more years of our veterans returning to broken-down barracks and substandard care. They need us to end a war that isn't making us safer. They need us to treat them with the care and respect they deserve. That's why I'm running for President.

The man I met in Pennsylvania who lost his job but can't even afford the gas to drive around and look for a new one – he can't afford four more years of an energy policy written by the oil companies and for the oil companies; a policy that's not only keeping gas at record prices, but funding both sides of the war on terror and destroying our planet in the process. He doesn't need four more years of Washington policies that sound good, but don't solve the problem. He needs us to take a permanent holiday from our oil addiction by making the automakers raise their fuel standards, corporations pay for their pollution, and oil companies invest their record profits in a clean energy future. That's the change we need. And that's why I'm running for President.

The people I've met in small towns and big cities across this country understand that government can't solve all our problems – and we don't expect it to. We believe in hard work. We believe in personal responsibility and self-reliance.

But we also believe that we have a larger responsibility to one another as Americans – that America is a place – that America is the place – where you can make it if you try. That no matter how much money you start with or where you come from or who your parents are, opportunity is yours if you're willing to reach for it and work for it. It's the idea that while there are few guarantees in life, you should be able to count on a job that pays the bills; health care for when you need it; a pension for when you retire; an education for your children that will allow them to fulfill their God-given potential. That's the America we believe in. That's the America I know.

This is the country that gave my grandfather a chance to go to college on the GI Bill when he came home from World War II; a country that gave him and my grandmother the chance to buy their first home with a loan from the government.

This is the country that made it possible for my mother – a single parent who had to go on food stamps at one point – to send my sister and me to the best schools in the country on scholarships.

This is the country that allowed my father-in-law – a city worker at a South Side water filtration plant – to provide for his wife and two children on a single salary. This is a man who was diagnosed at age thirty with multiple sclerosis – who relied on a walker to get himself to work. And yet, every day he went, and he labored, and he sent my wife and her brother to one of the best colleges in the nation. It was a job that didn't just give him a paycheck, but a sense of dignity and self-worth. It was an America that didn't just reward wealth, but the work and the workers who created it.

Somewhere along the way, between all the bickering and the influence-peddling and the game-playing of the last few decades, Washington and Wall Street have lost touch with these values. And while I honor John McCain's service to his country, his ideas for America are out of touch with these values. His plans for the future are nothing more than the failed policies of the past. And his plan to win in November appears to come from the very same playbook that his side has used time after time in election after election.

Yes, we know what's coming. We've seen it already. The same names and labels they always pin on everyone who doesn't agree with all their ideas. The same efforts to distract us from the issues that affect our lives by pouncing on every gaffe and association and fake controversy in the hope that the media will play along. The attempts to play on our fears and exploit our differences to turn us against each other for pure political gain – to slice and dice this country into Red States and Blue States; blue-collar and white-collar; white and black, and brown.

This is what they will do – no matter which one of us is the nominee. The question, then, is not what kind of campaign they'll run, it's what kind of campaign we will run. It's what we will do to make this year different. I didn't get into race thinking that I could avoid this kind of politics, but I am running for President because this is the time to end it.

We will end it this time not because I'm perfect – I think by now this campaign has reminded all of us of that. We will end it not by duplicating the same tactics and the same strategies as the other side, because that will just lead us down the same path of polarization and gridlock.

We will end it by telling the truth – forcefully, repeatedly, confidently – and by trusting that the American people will embrace the need for change.

Because that's how we've always changed this country – not from the top-down, but from the bottom-up; when you – the American people – decide that the stakes are too high and the challenges are too great.

The other side can label and name-call all they want, but I trust the American people to recognize that it's not surrender to end the war in Iraq so that we can rebuild our military and go after al Qaeda's leaders. I trust the American people to understand that it's not weakness, but wisdom to talk not just to our friends, but our enemies – like Roosevelt did, and Kennedy did, and Truman did.

I trust the American people to realize that while we don't need big government, we do need a government that stands up for families who are being tricked out of their homes by Wall Street predators; a government that stands up for the middle-class by giving them a tax break; a government that ensures that no American will ever lose their life savings just because their child gets sick. Security and opportunity; compassion and prosperity aren't liberal values or conservative values – they're American values.

Most of all, I trust the American people's desire to no longer be defined by our differences. Because no matter where I've been in this country – whether it was the corn fields of Iowa or the textile mills of the Carolinas; the streets of San Antonio or the foothills of Georgia –

I've found that while we may have different stories, we hold common hopes. We may not look the same or come from the same place, but we want to move in the same direction – towards a better future for our children and our grandchildren.

That's why I'm in this race. I love this country too much to see it divided and distracted at this moment in history. I believe in our ability to perfect this union because it's the only reason I'm standing here today. And I know the promise of America because I have lived it.

It is the light of opportunity that led my father across an ocean.

It is the founding ideals that the flag draped over my grandfather's coffin stands for – it is life, and liberty, and the pursuit of happiness.

It's the simple truth I learned all those years ago when I worked in the shadows of a shuttered steel mill on the South Side of Chicago – that in this country, justice can be won against the greatest of odds; hope can find its way back to the darkest of corners; and when we are told that we cannot bring about the change that we seek, we answer with one voice – yes we can.

So don't ever forget that this election is not about me, or any candidate. Don't ever forget that this campaign is about you – about your hopes, about your dreams, about your struggles, about securing your portion of the American Dream.

Don't ever forget that we have a choice in this country – that we can choose not to be divided; that we can choose not to be afraid; that we can still choose this moment to finally come together and solve the problems we've talked about all those other years in all those other elections.

This time can be different than all the rest. This time we can face down those who say our road is too long; that our climb is too steep; that we can no longer achieve the change that we seek. This is our time to answer the call that so many generations of Americans have answered before – by insisting that by hard work, and by sacrifice, the American Dream will endure. Thank you, and may God Bless the United States of America.

Final Primary Night – Presumptive Nominee Speech
St. Paul, Minnesota
June 3, 2008

Tonight, after fifty-four hard-fought contests, our primary season has finally come to an end.

Sixteen months have passed since we first stood together on the steps of the Old State Capitol in Springfield, Illinois. Thousands of miles have been traveled. Millions of voices have been heard. And because of what you said – because you decided that change must come to Washington; because you believed that this year must be different than all the rest; because you chose to listen not to your doubts or your fears but to your greatest hopes and highest aspirations, tonight we mark the end of one historic journey with the beginning of another – a journey that will bring a new and better day to America. Tonight, I can stand before you and say that I will be the Democratic nominee for President of the United States.

I want to thank every American who stood with us over the course of this campaign – through the good days and the bad; from the snows of Cedar Rapids to the sunshine of Sioux Falls. And tonight I also want to thank the men and woman who took this journey with me as fellow candidates for President.

At this defining moment for our nation, we should be proud that our party put forth one of the most talented, qualified field of individuals ever to run for this office. I have not just competed with them as rivals, I have learned from them as friends, as public servants, and as patriots who love America and are willing to work tirelessly to make this country better. They are leaders of this party, and leaders that America will turn to for years to come.

That is particularly true for the candidate who has traveled further on this journey than anyone else. Senator Hillary Clinton has made history in this campaign not just because she's a woman who has done what no woman has done before, but because she's a leader who inspires millions of Americans with her strength, her courage, and her commitment to the causes that brought us here tonight.

We've certainly had our differences over the last sixteen months. But as someone who's shared a stage with her many times, I can tell you that what gets Hillary Clinton up in the morning – even in the face of tough odds – is exactly what sent her and Bill Clinton to sign up for their first campaign in Texas all those years ago; what sent her to work at the Children's Defense Fund and made her fight for health care as First Lady; what led her to the United States Senate and fueled her barrier-breaking campaign for the presidency – an unyielding desire to improve the lives of ordinary Americans, no matter how difficult the fight may be. And you can rest assured that when we finally win the battle for universal health care in this country, she will be central to that victory. When we transform our energy policy and lift our children out of poverty, it will be because she worked to help make it happen. Our party and our country are better off because of her, and I am a better candidate for having had the honor to compete with Hillary Rodham Clinton.

There are those who say that this primary has somehow left us weaker and more divided. Well I say that because of this primary, there are millions of Americans who have cast their ballot for the very first time. There are Independents and Republicans who understand that this election isn't just about the party in charge of Washington, it's about the need to change Washington. There are young people, and African-Americans, and Latinos, and women of all ages who have voted in numbers that have broken records and inspired a nation.

All of you chose to support a candidate you believe in deeply. But at the end of the day, we aren't the reason you came out and waited in lines that stretched block after block to make your voice heard. You didn't do that because of me or Senator Clinton or anyone else. You did it because you know in your hearts that at this moment – a moment that will define a generation – we cannot afford to keep doing what we've been doing. We owe our children a better future. We owe our country a better future. And for all those who dream of that future tonight, I say – let us begin the work together. Let us unite in common effort to chart a new course for America.

In just a few short months, the Republican Party will arrive in St. Paul with a very different agenda. They will come here to nominate John McCain, a man who has served this country heroically. I honor that service, and I respect his many accomplishments, even if he chooses to deny mine. My differences with him are not personal; they are with the policies he has proposed in this campaign.

Because while John McCain can legitimately tout moments of independence from his party in the past, such independence has not been the hallmark of his presidential campaign.

It's not change when John McCain decided to stand with George Bush ninety-five percent of the time, as he did in the Senate last year.

It's not change when he offers four more years of Bush economic policies that have failed to create well-paying jobs, or insure our workers, or help Americans afford the skyrocketing cost of college – policies that have lowered the real incomes of the average American family, widened the gap between Wall Street and Main Street, and left our children with a mountain of debt.

And it's not change when he promises to continue a policy in Iraq that asks everything of our brave men and women in uniform and nothing of Iraqi politicians – a policy where all we look for are reasons to stay in Iraq, while we spend billions of dollars a month on a war that isn't making the American people any safer.

So I'll say this – there are many words to describe John McCain's attempt to pass off his embrace of George Bush's policies as bipartisan and new. But change is not one of them.

Change is a foreign policy that doesn't begin and end with a war that should've never been authorized and never been waged. I won't stand here and pretend that there are many good options left in Iraq, but what's not an option is leaving our troops in that country for the next hundred years – especially at a time when our military is overstretched, our nation is isolated, and nearly every other threat to

America is being ignored.

We must be as careful getting out of Iraq as we were careless getting in - but start leaving we must. It's time for Iraqis to take responsibility for their future. It's time to rebuild our military and give our veterans the care they need and the benefits they deserve when they come home. It's time to refocus our efforts on al Qaeda's leadership and Afghanistan, and rally the world against the common threats of the 21st century – terrorism and nuclear weapons; climate change and poverty; genocide and disease. That's what change is.

Change is realizing that meeting today's threats requires not just our firepower, but the power of our diplomacy – tough, direct diplomacy where the President of the United States isn't afraid to let any petty dictator know where America stands and what we stand for. We must once again have the courage and conviction to lead the free world. That is the legacy of Roosevelt, and Truman, and Kennedy. That's what the American people want. That's what change is.

Change is building an economy that rewards not just wealth, but the work and workers who created it. It's understanding that the struggles facing working families can't be solved by spending billions of dollars on more tax breaks for big corporations and wealthy CEOs, but by giving a the middle-class a tax break, and investing in our crumbling infrastructure, and transforming how we use energy, and improving our schools, and renewing our commitment to science and innovation. It's understanding that fiscal responsibility and shared prosperity can go hand-in-hand, as they did when Bill Clinton was

President.

John McCain has spent a lot of time talking about trips to Iraq in the last few weeks, but maybe if he spent some time taking trips to the cities and towns that have been hardest hit by this economy – cities in Michigan, and Ohio, and right here in Minnesota – he'd understand the kind of change that people are looking for.

Maybe if he went to Iowa and met the student who works the night shift after a full day of class and still can't pay the medical bills for a sister who's ill, he'd understand that she can't afford four more years of a health care plan that only takes care of the healthy and wealthy. She needs us to pass health care plan that guarantees insurance to every American who wants it and brings down premiums for every family who needs it. That's the change we need.

Maybe if he went to Pennsylvania and met the man who lost his job but can't even afford the gas to drive around and look for a new one, he'd understand that we can't afford four more years of our addiction to oil from dictators. That man needs us to pass an energy policy that works with automakers to raise fuel standards, and makes corporations pay for their pollution, and oil companies invest their record profits in a clean energy future – an energy policy that will create millions of new jobs that pay well and can't be outsourced. That's the change we need.

And maybe if he spent some time in the schools of South Carolina or St. Paul or where he spoke tonight in New Orleans, he'd understand that we can't afford to leave the money behind for No

Child Left Behind; that we owe it to our children to invest in early childhood education; to recruit an army of new teachers and give them better pay and more support; to finally decide that in this global economy, the chance to get a college education should not be a privilege for the wealthy few, but the birthright of every American. That's the change we need in America. That's why I'm running for President.

The other side will come here in September and offer a very different set of policies and positions, and that is a debate I look forward to. It is a debate the American people deserve. But what you don't deserve is another election that's governed by fear, and innuendo, and division. What you won't hear from this campaign or this party is the kind of politics that uses religion as a wedge, and patriotism as a bludgeon – that sees our opponents not as competitors to challenge, but enemies to demonize. Because we may call ourselves Democrats and Republicans, but we are Americans first. We are always Americans first.

Despite what the good Senator from Arizona said tonight, I have seen people of differing views and opinions find common cause many times during my two decades in public life, and I have brought many together myself. I've walked arm-in-arm with community leaders on the South Side of Chicago and watched tensions fade as black, white, and Latino fought together for good jobs and good schools. I've sat across the table from law enforcement and civil rights advocates to reform a criminal justice system that sent thirteen innocent people to death row. And I've worked with friends in the other party to provide more children with health insurance and more working families with a tax break; to curb the spread of nuclear weapons and ensure that the American people know where their tax dollars are being spent; and to reduce the influence of lobbyists who have all too often set the agenda in Washington.

In our country, I have found that this cooperation happens not because we agree on everything, but because behind all the labels and false divisions and categories that define us; beyond all the petty bickering and point-scoring in Washington, Americans are a decent, generous, compassionate people, united by common challenges and common hopes. And every so often, there are moments which call on that fundamental goodness to make this country great again.

So it was for that band of patriots who declared in a Philadelphia hall the formation of a more perfect union; and for all those who gave on the fields of Gettysburg and Antietam their last full measure of devotion to save that same union.

So it was for the Greatest Generation that conquered fear itself, and liberated a continent from tyranny, and made this country home to untold opportunity and prosperity.

So it was for the workers who stood out on the picket lines; the women who shattered glass ceilings; the children who braved a Selma bridge for freedom's cause.

So it has been for every generation that faced down the greatest challenges and the most improbable odds to leave their children a world that's better, and kinder, and more just.

And so it must be for us.

America, this is our moment. This is our time. Our time to turn the page on the policies of the past. Our time to bring new energy and new ideas to the challenges we face. Our time to offer a new direction for the country we love.

The journey will be difficult. The road will be long. I face this challenge with profound humility, and knowledge of my own limitations. But I also face it with limitless faith in the capacity of the American people. Because if we are willing to work for it, and fight for it, and believe in it, then I am absolutely certain that generations from now, we will be able to look back and tell our children that this was the moment when we began to provide care for the sick and good jobs to the jobless; this was the moment when the rise of the oceans began to slow and our planet began to heal; this was the moment when we ended a war and secured our nation and restored our image as the last, best hope on Earth. This was the moment – this was the time – when we came together to remake this great nation so that it may always reflect our very best selves, and our highest ideals. Thank you, God Bless you, and may God Bless the United States of America.

A World that Stands as One
July 24th, 2008
Berlin, Germany

Thank you to the citizens of Berlin and to the people of Germany. Let me thank Chancellor Merkel and Foreign Minister Steinmeier for welcoming me earlier today. Thank you Mayor Wowereit, the Berlin Senate, the police, and most of all thank you for this welcome.

I come to Berlin as so many of my countrymen have come before. Tonight, I speak to you not as a candidate for President, but as a citizen — a proud citizen of the United States, and a fellow citizen of the world.

I know that I don't look like the Americans who've previously spoken in this great city. The journey that led me here is improbable. My mother was born in the heartland of America, but my father grew up herding goats in Kenya. His father - my grandfather - was a cook, a domestic servant to the British.

At the height of the Cold War, my father decided, like so many others in the forgotten corners of the world, that his yearning - his dream - required the freedom and opportunity promised by the West. And so he wrote letter after letter to universities all across America until somebody, somewhere answered his prayer for a better life.

That is why I'm here. And you are here because you too know that yearning. This city, of all cities, knows the dream of freedom. And you know that the only reason we stand here tonight is because men and women from both of our nations came together to work, and struggle, and sacrifice for that better life.

Ours is a partnership that truly began sixty years ago this summer, on the day when the first American plane touched down at Templehof.

On that day, much of this continent still lay in ruin. The rubble of this city had yet to be built into a wall. The Soviet shadow had swept across Eastern Europe, while in the West, America, Britain, and France took stock of their losses, and pondered how the world might be remade.

This is where the two sides met. And on the twenty-fourth of June, 1948, the Communists chose to blockade the western part of the city. They cut off food and supplies to more than two million Germans in an effort to extinguish the last flame of freedom in Berlin.

The size of our forces was no match for the much larger Soviet Army. And yet retreat would have allowed Communism to march across Europe. Where the last war had ended, another World War could have easily begun. All that stood in the way was Berlin.

And that's when the airlift began - when the largest and most unlikely rescue in history brought food and hope to the people of this city.

The odds were stacked against success. In the winter, a heavy fog filled the sky above, and many planes were forced to turn back without dropping off the needed supplies. The streets where we stand were filled with hungry families who had no comfort from the cold.

But in the darkest hours, the people of Berlin kept the flame of hope burning. The people of Berlin refused to give up. And on one fall day, hundreds of thousands of Berliners came here, to the Tiergarten, and heard the city's mayor implore the world not to give up on freedom. "There is only one possibility," he said. "For us to stand together united until this battle is won...The people of Berlin have spoken. We have done our duty, and we will keep on doing our duty. People of the world: now do your duty...People of the world, look at Berlin!"

People of the world - look at Berlin!

Look at Berlin, where Germans and Americans learned to work together and trust each other less than three years after facing each other on the field of battle.

Look at Berlin, where the determination of a people met the generosity of the Marshall Plan and created a German miracle; where a victory over tyranny gave rise to NATO, the greatest alliance ever formed to defend our common security.

Look at Berlin, where the bullet holes in the buildings and the somber stones and pillars near the Brandenburg Gate insist that we never forget our common humanity.

People of the world - look at Berlin, where a wall came down, a continent came together, and history proved that there is no challenge too great for a world that stands as one.

Sixty years after the airlift, we are called upon again. History has led us to a new crossroad, with new promise and new peril. When you, the German people, tore down that wall - a wall that divided East and West; freedom and tyranny; fear and hope - walls came tumbling down around the world. From Kiev to Cape Town, prison camps were closed, and the doors of democracy were opened. Markets opened too, and the spread of information and technology reduced barriers to opportunity and prosperity. While the 20th century taught us that we share a common destiny, the 21st has revealed a world more intertwined than at any time in human history.

The fall of the Berlin Wall brought new hope. But that very closeness has given rise to new dangers - dangers that cannot be contained within the borders of a country or by the distance of an ocean.

The terrorists of September 11th plotted in Hamburg and trained in Kandahar and Karachi before killing thousands from all over the globe on American soil.

As we speak, cars in Boston and factories in Beijing are melting the ice caps in the Arctic, shrinking coastlines in the Atlantic, and bringing drought to farms from Kansas to Kenya.

Poorly secured nuclear material in the former Soviet Union, or secrets from a scientist in Pakistan could help build a bomb that detonates in Paris. The poppies in Afghanistan become the heroin in Berlin. The poverty and violence in Somalia breeds the terror of tomorrow. The genocide in Darfur shames the conscience of us all.

In this new world, such dangerous currents have swept along faster than our efforts to contain them. That is why we cannot afford to be divided. No one nation, no matter how large or powerful, can defeat such challenges alone. None of us can deny these threats, or escape responsibility in meeting them. Yet, in the absence of Soviet tanks and a terrible wall, it has become easy to forget this truth. And if we're honest with each other, we know that sometimes, on both sides of the Atlantic, we have drifted apart, and forgotten our shared destiny.

In Europe, the view that America is part of what has gone wrong in our world, rather than a force to help make it right, has become all too common. In America, there are voices that deride and deny the importance of Europe's role in our security and our future. Both views miss the truth - that Europeans today are bearing new burdens and taking more responsibility in critical parts of the world; and that just as American bases built in the last century still help to defend the security of this continent, so does our country still sacrifice greatly for freedom around the globe.

Yes, there have been differences between America and Europe. No doubt, there will be differences in the future. But the burdens of global citizenship continue to bind us together. A change of leadership in Washington will not lift this burden. In this new century, Americans and Europeans alike will be required to do more - not less. Partnership and cooperation among nations is not a choice; it is the one way, the only way, to protect our common security and advance our common humanity.

That is why the greatest danger of all is to allow new walls to divide us from one another.

The walls between old allies on either side of the Atlantic cannot stand. The walls between the countries with the most and those with the least cannot stand. The walls between races and tribes; natives and immigrants; Christian and Muslim and Jew cannot stand. These now are the walls we must tear down.

We know they have fallen before. After centuries of strife, the people of Europe have formed a Union of promise and prosperity. Here, at the base of a column built to mark victory in war, we meet in the center of a Europe at peace. Not only have walls come down in Berlin, but they have come down in Belfast, where Protestant and Catholic found a way to live together; in the Balkans, where our Atlantic alliance ended wars and brought savage war criminals to justice; and in South Africa, where the struggle of a courageous people defeated apartheid.

So history reminds us that walls can be torn down. But the task is never easy. True partnership and true progress requires constant work and sustained sacrifice. They require sharing the burdens of development and diplomacy; of progress and peace. They require allies who will listen to each other, learn from each other and, most of all, trust each other.

That is why America cannot turn inward. That is why Europe cannot turn inward. America has no better partner than Europe. Now is the time to build new bridges across the globe as strong as the one that bound us across the Atlantic. Now is the time to join together, through constant cooperation, strong institutions, shared sacrifice, and a global commitment to progress, to meet the challenges of the 21st century. It was this spirit that led airlift planes to appear in the sky above our heads, and people to assemble where we stand today. And this is the moment when our nations - and all nations - must summon that spirit anew.

This is the moment when we must defeat terror and dry up the well of extremism that supports it. This threat is real and we cannot shrink from our responsibility to combat it. If we could create NATO to face down the Soviet Union, we can join in a new and global partnership to dismantle the networks that have struck in Madrid and Amman; in London and Bali; in Washington and New York. If we could win a battle of ideas against the communists, we can stand with the vast majority of Muslims who reject the extremism that leads to hate instead of hope.

This is the moment when we must renew our resolve to rout the terrorists who threaten our security in Afghanistan, and the traffickers who sell drugs on your streets. No one welcomes war. I recognize the enormous difficulties in Afghanistan. But my country and yours have a stake in seeing that NATO's first mission beyond Europe's borders is a success. For the people of Afghanistan, and for our shared security, the work must be done. America cannot do this alone. The Afghan people need our troops and your troops; our support and your support to defeat the Taliban and al Qaeda, to develop their economy, and to help them rebuild their nation. We have too much at stake to turn back now.

This is the moment when we must renew the goal of a world without nuclear weapons. The two superpowers that faced each other across the wall of this city came too close too often to destroying all we have built and all that we love. With that wall gone, we need not stand idly by and watch the further spread of the deadly atom. It is time to secure all loose nuclear materials; to stop the spread of nuclear weapons; and to reduce the arsenals from another era. This is the moment to begin the work of seeking the peace of a world without nuclear weapons.

This is the moment when every nation in Europe must have the chance to choose its own tomorrow free from the shadows of yesterday. In this century, we need a strong European Union that deepens the security and prosperity of this continent, while extending a hand abroad. In this century - in this city of all cities - we must reject the Cold War mind-set of the past, and resolve to work with Russia when we can, to stand up for our values when we must, and to seek a partnership that extends across this entire continent.

This is the moment when we must build on the wealth that open markets have created, and share its benefits more equitably. Trade has been a cornerstone of our growth and global development. But we will not be able to sustain this growth if it favors the few, and not the many. Together, we must forge trade that truly rewards the work that creates wealth, with meaningful protections for our people and our planet. This is the moment for trade that is free and fair for all.

This is the moment we must help answer the call for a new dawn in the Middle East. My country must stand with yours and with Europe in sending a direct message to Iran that it must abandon its nuclear ambitions. We must support the Lebanese who have marched and bled for democracy, and the Israelis and Palestinians who seek a secure and lasting peace. And despite past differences, this is the moment when the world should support the millions of Iraqis who seek to rebuild their lives, even as we pass responsibility to the Iraqi government and finally bring this war to a close.

This is the moment when we must come together to save this planet. Let us resolve that we will not leave our children a world where the oceans rise and famine spreads and terrible storms devastate our lands. Let us resolve that all nations - including my own - will act with the same seriousness of purpose as has your nation, and reduce the carbon we send into our atmosphere. This is the moment to give our children back their future. This is the moment to stand as one.

And this is the moment when we must give hope to those left behind in a globalized world. We must remember that the Cold War born in this city was not a battle for land or treasure. Sixty years ago, the planes that flew over Berlin did not drop bombs; instead they delivered food, and coal, and candy to grateful children. And in that show of solidarity, those pilots won more than a military victory. They won hearts and minds; love and loyalty and trust - not just from the people in this city, but from all those who heard the story of what they did here.

Now the world will watch and remember what we do here - what we do with this moment. Will we extend our hand to the people in the forgotten corners of this world who yearn for lives marked by dignity and opportunity; by security and justice? Will we lift the child in Bangladesh from poverty, shelter the refugee in Chad, and banish the scourge of AIDS in our time?

Will we stand for the human rights of the dissident in Burma, the blogger in Iran, or the voter in Zimbabwe? Will we give meaning to the words "never again" in Darfur?

Will we acknowledge that there is no more powerful example than the one each of our nations projects to the world? Will we reject torture and stand for the rule of law? Will we welcome immigrants from different lands, and shun discrimination against those who don't look like us or worship like we do, and keep the promise of equality and opportunity for all of our people?

People of Berlin - people of the world - this is our moment. This is our time.

I know my country has not perfected itself. At times, we've struggled to keep the promise of liberty and equality for all of our people. We've made our share of mistakes, and there are times when our actions around the world have not lived up to our best intentions.

But I also know how much I love America. I know that for more than two centuries, we have strived - at great cost and great sacrifice - to form a more perfect union; to seek, with other nations, a more hopeful world. Our allegiance has never been to any particular tribe or kingdom - indeed, every language is spoken in our country; every culture has left its imprint on ours; every point of view is expressed in our public squares. What has always united us - what has always driven our people; what drew my father to America's shores - is a set of ideals that speak to aspirations shared by all people: that we can live free from fear and free from want; that we can speak our minds and assemble with whomever we choose and worship as we please.

These are the aspirations that joined the fates of all nations in this city. These aspirations are bigger than anything that drives us apart. It is because of these aspirations that the airlift began. It is because of these aspirations that all free people - everywhere - became citizens of Berlin. It is in pursuit of these aspirations that a new generation - our generation - must make our mark on the world.

People of Berlin - and people of the world - the scale of our challenge is great. The road ahead will be long. But I come before you to say that we are heirs to a struggle for freedom. We are a people of improbable hope. With an eye toward the future, with resolve in our hearts, let us remember this history, and answer our destiny, and remake the world once again.

The American Promise
Acceptance Speech at the Democratic Convention
Mile High Stadium
August 28, 2008

To Chairman Dean and my great friend Dick Durbin; and to all my fellow citizens of this great nation;

With profound gratitude and great humility, I accept your nomination for the presidency of the United States.

Let me express my thanks to the historic slate of candidates who accompanied me on this journey, and especially the one who traveled the farthest - a champion for working Americans and an inspiration to my daughters and to yours -- Hillary Rodham Clinton. To President Clinton, who last night made the case for change as only he can make it; to Ted Kennedy, who embodies the spirit of service; and to the next Vice President of the United States, Joe Biden, I thank you. I am grateful to finish this journey with one of the finest statesmen of our time, a man at ease with everyone from world leaders to the conductors on the Amtrak train he still takes home every night.

To the love of my life, our next First Lady, Michelle Obama, and to Sasha and Malia - I love you so much, and I'm so proud of all of you.

Four years ago, I stood before you and told you my story - of the brief union between a young man from Kenya and a young woman from Kansas who weren't well-off or well-known, but shared a belief that in America, their son could achieve whatever he put his mind to.

It is that promise that has always set this country apart - that through hard work and sacrifice, each of us can pursue our individual dreams but still come together as one American family, to ensure that the next generation can pursue their dreams as well.

That's why I stand here tonight. Because for two hundred and thirty two years, at each moment when that promise was in jeopardy, ordinary men and women - students and soldiers, farmers and teachers, nurses and janitors -- found the courage to keep it alive.

We meet at one of those defining moments - a moment when our nation is at war, our economy is in turmoil, and the American promise has been threatened once more.

Tonight, more Americans are out of work and more are working harder for less. More of you have lost your homes and even more are watching your home values plummet. More of you have cars you can't afford to drive, credit card bills you can't afford to pay, and tuition that's beyond your reach.

These challenges are not all of government's making. But the failure to respond is a direct result of a broken politics in Washington and the failed policies of George W. Bush.

America, we are better than these last eight years. We are a better country than this.

This country is more decent than one where a woman in Ohio, on the brink of retirement, finds herself one illness away from disaster after a lifetime of hard work.

This country is more generous than one where a man in Indiana has to pack up the equipment he's worked on for twenty years and watch it shipped off to China, and then chokes up as he explains how he felt like a failure when he went home to tell his family the news.

We are more compassionate than a government that lets veterans sleep on our streets and families slide into poverty; that sits on its hands while a major American city drowns before our eyes.

Tonight, I say to the American people, to Democrats and Republicans and Independents across this great land - enough! This moment - this election - is our chance to keep, in the 21st century, the American promise alive. Because next week, in Minnesota, the same party that brought you two terms of George Bush and Dick Cheney will ask this country for a third. And we are here because we love this country too much to let the next four years look like the last eight. On November 4th, we must stand up and say: "Eight is enough."

Now let there be no doubt. The Republican nominee, John McCain, has worn the uniform of our country with bravery and distinction, and for that we owe him our gratitude and respect. And next week, we'll also hear about those occasions when he's broken with his party as evidence that he can deliver the change that we need.

But the record's clear: John McCain has voted with George Bush ninety percent of the time. Senator McCain likes to talk about judgment, but really, what does it say about your judgment when you think George Bush has been right more than ninety percent of the time? I don't know about you, but I'm not ready to take a ten percent chance on change.

The truth is, on issue after issue that would make a difference in your lives - on health care and education and the economy - Senator McCain has been anything but independent. He said that our economy has made "great progress" under this President. He said that the fundamentals of the economy are strong. And when one of his chief advisors - the man who wrote his economic plan - was talking about the anxiety Americans are feeling, he said that we were just suffering from a "mental recession," and that we've become, and I quote, "a nation of whiners."

A nation of whiners? Tell that to the proud auto workers at a Michigan plant who, after they found out it was closing, kept showing up every day and working as hard as ever, because they knew there were people who counted on the brakes that they made. Tell that to the military families who shoulder their burdens silently as they watch their loved ones leave for their third or fourth or fifth tour of duty. These are not whiners. They work hard and give back and keep going without complaint. These are the Americans that I know.

Now, I don't believe that Senator McCain doesn't care what's going on in the lives of Americans. I just think he doesn't know. Why else would he define middle-class as someone making under five million dollars a year? How else could he propose hundreds of billions in tax breaks for big corporations and oil companies but not one penny of tax relief to more than one hundred million Americans? How else could he offer a health care plan that would actually tax people's benefits, or an education plan that would do nothing to help families pay for college, or a plan that would privatize Social Security and gamble your retirement?

It's not because John McCain doesn't care. It's because John McCain doesn't get it.

For over two decades, he's subscribed to that old, discredited Republican philosophy - give more and more to those with the most and hope that prosperity trickles down to everyone else. In Washington, they call this the Ownership Society, but what it really means is - you're on your own. Out of work? Tough luck. No health care? The market will fix it. Born into poverty? Pull yourself up by your own bootstraps - even if you don't have boots. You're on your own.

Well it's time for them to own their failure. It's time for us to change America.

You see, we Democrats have a very different measure of what constitutes progress in this country.

We measure progress by how many people can find a job that pays the mortgage; whether you can put a little extra money away at the end of each month so you can someday watch your child receive her college diploma. We measure progress in the 23 million new jobs that were created when Bill Clinton was President - when the average American family saw its income go up $7,500 instead of down $2,000 like it has under George Bush.

We measure the strength of our economy not by the number of billionaires we have or the profits of the Fortune 500, but by whether someone with a good idea can take a risk and start a new business, or whether the waitress who lives on tips can take a day off to look after a sick kid without losing her job - an economy that honors the dignity of work.

The fundamentals we use to measure economic strength are whether we are living up to that fundamental promise that has made this country great - a promise that is the only reason I am standing here tonight.

Because in the faces of those young veterans who come back from Iraq and Afghanistan, I see my grandfather, who signed up after Pearl Harbor, marched in Patton's Army, and was rewarded by a grateful nation with the chance to go to college on the GI Bill.

In the face of that young student who sleeps just three hours before working the night shift, I think about my mom, who raised my sister and me on her own while she worked and earned her degree; who once turned to food stamps but was still able to send us to the best schools in the country with the help of student loans and scholarships.

When I listen to another worker tell me that his factory has shut down, I remember all those men and women on the South Side of Chicago who I stood by and fought for two decades ago after the local steel plant closed.

And when I hear a woman talk about the difficulties of starting her own business, I think about my grandmother, who worked her way up from the secretarial pool to middle-management, despite years of being passed over for promotions because she was a woman. She's the one who taught me about hard work. She's the one who put off buying a new car or a new dress for herself so that I could have a better life. She poured everything she had into me. And although she can no longer travel, I know that she's watching tonight, and that tonight is her night as well.

I don't know what kind of lives John McCain thinks that celebrities lead, but this has been mine. These are my heroes. Theirs are the stories that shaped me. And it is on their behalf that I intend to win this election and keep our promise alive as President of the United States.

What is that promise?

It's a promise that says each of us has the freedom to make of our own lives what we will, but that we also have the obligation to treat each other with dignity and respect.

It's a promise that says the market should reward drive and innovation and generate growth, but that businesses should live up to their responsibilities to create American jobs, look out for American workers, and play by the rules of the road.

Ours is a promise that says government cannot solve all our problems, but what it should do is that which we cannot do for ourselves - protect us from harm and provide every child a decent education; keep our water clean and our toys safe; invest in new schools and new roads and new science and technology.

Our government should work for us, not against us. It should help us, not hurt us. It should ensure opportunity not just for those with the most money and influence, but for every American who's willing to work.

That's the promise of America - the idea that we are responsible for ourselves, but that we also rise or fall as one nation; the fundamental belief that I am my brother's keeper; I am my sister's keeper.

That's the promise we need to keep. That's the change we need right now. So let me spell out exactly what that change would mean if I am President.

Change means a tax code that doesn't reward the lobbyists who wrote it, but the American workers and small businesses who deserve it.

Unlike John McCain, I will stop giving tax breaks to corporations that ship jobs overseas, and I will start giving them to companies that create good jobs right here in America.

I will eliminate capital gains taxes for the small businesses and the start-ups that will create the high-wage, high-tech jobs of tomorrow.

I will cut taxes - cut taxes - for 95% of all working families. Because in an economy like this, the last thing we should do is raise taxes on the middle-class.

And for the sake of our economy, our security, and the future of our planet, I will set a clear goal as President: in ten years, we will finally end our dependence on oil from the Middle East.

Washington's been talking about our oil addiction for the last thirty years, and John McCain has been there for twenty-six of them. In that time, he's said no to higher fuel-efficiency standards for cars, no to investments in renewable energy, no to renewable fuels. And today, we import triple the amount of oil as the day that Senator McCain took office.

Now is the time to end this addiction, and to understand that drilling is a stop-gap measure, not a long-term solution. Not even close.

As President, I will tap our natural gas reserves, invest in clean coal technology, and find ways to safely harness nuclear power. I'll help our auto companies re-tool, so that the fuel-efficient cars of the future are built right here in America. I'll make it easier for the American people to afford these new cars. And I'll invest 150 billion dollars over the next decade in affordable, renewable sources of energy - wind power and solar power and the next generation of biofuels; an investment that will lead to new industries and five million new jobs that pay well and can't ever be outsourced.

America, now is not the time for small plans.

Now is the time to finally meet our moral obligation to provide every child a world-class education, because it will take nothing less to compete in the global economy. Michelle and I are only here tonight because we were given a chance at an education. And I will not settle for an America where some kids don't have that chance. I'll invest in early childhood education. I'll recruit an army of new teachers, and pay them higher salaries and give them more support. And in exchange, I'll ask for higher standards and more accountability. And we will keep our promise to every young American - if you commit to serving your community or your country, we will make sure you can afford a college education.

Now is the time to finally keep the promise of affordable, accessible health care for every single American. If you have health care, my plan will lower your premiums. If you don't, you'll be able to get the same kind of coverage that members of Congress give themselves. And as someone who watched my mother argue with insurance companies while she lay in bed dying of cancer, I will make certain those companies stop discriminating against those who are sick and need care the most.

Now is the time to help families with paid sick days and better family leave, because nobody in America should have to choose between keeping their jobs and caring for a sick child or ailing parent.

Now is the time to change our bankruptcy laws, so that your pensions are protected ahead of CEO bonuses; and the time to protect Social Security for future generations.

And now is the time to keep the promise of equal pay for an equal day's work, because I want my daughters to have exactly the same opportunities as your sons.

Now, many of these plans will cost money, which is why I've laid out how I'll pay for every dime - by closing corporate loopholes and tax havens that don't help America grow. But I will also go through the federal budget, line by line, eliminating programs that no longer work and making the ones we do need work better and cost less - because we cannot meet twenty-first century challenges with a twentieth century bureaucracy.

And Democrats, we must also admit that fulfilling America's promise will require more than just money. It will require a renewed sense of responsibility from each of us to recover what John F. Kennedy called our "intellectual and moral strength." Yes, government must lead on energy independence, but each of us must do our part to make our homes and businesses more efficient. Yes, we must provide more ladders to success for young men who fall into lives of crime and despair. But we must also admit that programs alone can't replace parents; that government can't turn off the television and make a child do her homework; that fathers must take more responsibility for providing the love and guidance their children need.

Individual responsibility and mutual responsibility - that's the essence of America's promise.

And just as we keep our keep our promise to the next generation here at home, so must we keep America's promise abroad. If John McCain wants to have a debate about who has the temperament, and judgment, to serve as the next Commander-in-Chief, that's a debate I'm ready to have.

For while Senator McCain was turning his sights to Iraq just days after 9/11, I stood up and opposed this war, knowing that it would distract us from the real threats we face. When John McCain said we could just "muddle through" in Afghanistan, I argued for more resources and more troops to finish the fight against the terrorists who actually attacked us on 9/11, and made clear that we must take out Osama bin Laden and his lieutenants if we have them in our sights. John McCain likes to say that he'll follow bin Laden to the Gates of Hell - but he won't even go to the cave where he lives.

And today, as my call for a time frame to remove our troops from Iraq has been echoed by the Iraqi government and even the Bush Administration, even after we learned that Iraq has a $79 billion surplus while we're wallowing in deficits, John McCain stands alone in his stubborn refusal to end a misguided war.

That's not the judgment we need. That won't keep America safe. We need a President who can face the threats of the future, not keep grasping at the ideas of the past.

You don't defeat a terrorist network that operates in eighty countries by occupying Iraq. You don't protect Israel and deter Iran just by talking tough in Washington. You can't truly stand up for Georgia when you've strained our oldest alliances. If John McCain wants to follow George Bush with more tough talk and bad strategy, that is his choice - but it is not the change we need.

We are the party of Roosevelt. We are the party of Kennedy. So don't tell me that Democrats won't defend this country. Don't tell me that Democrats won't keep us safe. The Bush-McCain foreign policy has squandered the legacy that generations of Americans --

Democrats and Republicans - have built, and we are here to restore that legacy.

As Commander-in-Chief, I will never hesitate to defend this nation, but I will only send our troops into harm's way with a clear mission and a sacred commitment to give them the equipment they need in battle and the care and benefits they deserve when they come home.

I will end this war in Iraq responsibly, and finish the fight against al Qaeda and the Taliban in Afghanistan. I will rebuild our military to meet future conflicts. But I will also renew the tough, direct diplomacy that can prevent Iran from obtaining nuclear weapons and curb Russian aggression. I will build new partnerships to defeat the threats of the 21st century: terrorism and nuclear proliferation; poverty and genocide; climate change and disease. And I will restore our moral standing, so that America is once again that last, best hope for all who are called to the cause of freedom, who long for lives of peace, and who yearn for a better future.

These are the policies I will pursue. And in the weeks ahead, I look forward to debating them with John McCain.

But what I will not do is suggest that the Senator takes his positions for political purposes. Because one of the things that we have to change in our politics is the idea that people cannot disagree without challenging each other's character and patriotism.

The times are too serious, the stakes are too high for this same partisan playbook. So let us agree that patriotism has no party. I love this country, and so do you, and so does John McCain. The men and women who serve in our battlefields may be Democrats and Republicans and Independents, but they have fought together and bled together and some died together under the same proud flag. They have not served a Red America or a Blue America - they have served the United States of America.

So I've got news for you, John McCain. We all put our country first.

America, our work will not be easy. The challenges we face require tough choices, and Democrats as well as Republicans will need to cast off the worn-out ideas and politics of the past. For part of what has been lost these past eight years can't just be measured by lost wages or bigger trade deficits. What has also been lost is our sense of common purpose - our sense of higher purpose. And that's what we have to restore.

We may not agree on abortion, but surely we can agree on reducing the number of unwanted pregnancies in this country. The reality of gun ownership may be different for hunters in rural Ohio than for those plagued by gang-violence in Cleveland, but don't tell me we can't uphold the Second Amendment while keeping AK-47s out of the hands of criminals. I know there are differences on same-sex marriage, but surely we can agree that our gay and lesbian brothers and sisters deserve to visit the person they love in the hospital and to live lives free of discrimination. Passions fly on immigration, but I don't know anyone who benefits when a mother is separated from her infant child or an employer undercuts American wages by hiring illegal workers. This too is part of America's promise - the promise of a democracy where we can find the strength and grace to bridge divides and unite in common effort.

I know there are those who dismiss such beliefs as happy talk. They claim that our insistence on something larger, something firmer and more honest in our public life is just a Trojan Horse for higher taxes and the abandonment of traditional values. And that's to be expected. Because if you don't have any fresh ideas, then you use stale tactics to scare the voters. If you don't have a record to run on, then you paint your opponent as someone people should run from.

You make a big election about small things.

And you know what - it's worked before. Because it feeds into the cynicism we all have about government. When Washington doesn't work, all its promises seem empty. If your hopes have been dashed again and again, then it's best to stop hoping, and settle for what you already know.

I get it. I realize that I am not the likeliest candidate for this office. I don't fit the typical pedigree, and I haven't spent my career in the halls of Washington.

But I stand before you tonight because all across America something is stirring. What the nay-sayers don't understand is that this election has never been about me. It's been about you.

For eighteen long months, you have stood up, one by one, and said enough to the politics of the past. You understand that in this election, the greatest risk we can take is to try the same old politics with the same old players and expect a different result. You have shown what history teaches us - that at defining moments like this one, the change we need doesn't come from Washington. Change comes to Washington. Change happens because the American people demand it - because they rise up and insist on new ideas and new leadership, a new politics for a new time.

America, this is one of those moments.

I believe that as hard as it will be, the change we need is coming. Because I've seen it. Because I've lived it. I've seen it in Illinois, when we provided health care to more children and moved more families from welfare to work. I've seen it in Washington, when we worked across party lines to open up government and hold lobbyists more accountable, to give better care for our veterans and keep nuclear weapons out of terrorist hands.

And I've seen it in this campaign. In the young people who voted for the first time, and in those who got involved again after a very long time. In the Republicans who never thought they'd pick up a Democratic ballot, but did. I've seen it in the workers who would rather cut their hours back a day than see their friends lose their jobs, in the soldiers who re-enlist after losing a limb, in the good neighbors who take a stranger in when a hurricane strikes and the floodwaters rise.

This country of ours has more wealth than any nation, but that's not what makes us rich. We have the most powerful military on

Earth, but that's not what makes us strong. Our universities and our culture are the envy of the world, but that's not what keeps the world coming to our shores.

Instead, it is that American spirit - that American promise - that pushes us forward even when the path is uncertain; that binds us together in spite of our differences; that makes us fix our eye not on what is seen, but what is unseen, that better place around the bend.

That promise is our greatest inheritance. It's a promise I make to my daughters when I tuck them in at night, and a promise that you make to yours - a promise that has led immigrants to cross oceans and pioneers to travel west; a promise that led workers to picket lines, and women to reach for the ballot.

And it is that promise that forty five years ago today, brought Americans from every corner of this land to stand together on a Mall in Washington, before Lincoln's Memorial, and hear a young preacher from Georgia speak of his dream.

The men and women who gathered there could've heard many things. They could've heard words of anger and discord. They could've been told to succumb to the fear and frustration of so many dreams deferred.

But what the people heard instead - people of every creed and color, from every walk of life - is that in America, our destiny is inextricably linked. That together, our dreams can be one.

"We cannot walk alone," the preacher cried. "And as we walk, we must make the pledge that we shall always march ahead. We cannot turn back."

America, we cannot turn back. Not with so much work to be done. Not with so many children to educate, and so many veterans to care for. Not with an economy to fix and cities to rebuild and farms to save. Not with so many families to protect and so many lives to mend. America, we cannot turn back. We cannot walk alone. At this moment, in this election, we must pledge once more to march into the future. Let us keep that promise - that American promise - and in the words of Scripture hold firmly, without wavering, to the hope that we confess.

Thank you, and God Bless the United States of America.

Manassas, Prince William County, Virginia
November 3, 2008
10:30pm – Night Before the Election
Estimated Crowd: 100,000+

What a scene. What a crowd. Thank you for Virginia. (Crowd chants "yes we can.")

Let me start by noting, Virginia that this is our last rally. This is the last rally of a campaign that began nearly 2 years ago. We've gone to every corner of this country, from here in Northern Virginia to the rocky coasts of Maine, to the open plains of Texas, to the open skies of Montana.

I just want to say that whatever happens tomorrow, I have been deeply humbled by this journey. You have welcomed Michelle and me and the girls into your homes. You have shared your stories of struggle, you have spoken of your dreams, along the way, talking with all of you about your own lives.

You have enriched my life, you have moved me again and again. You have inspired me. Sometimes when I have been down you have lifted me up. You filled me with new hope for our future and you have reminded me about what makes America so special. In the places I have gone and the people I have met, I have been struck again and again by the fundamental decency and generosity and dignity of men and women who work hard without complaint, to meet their responsibilities every day.

I come away with an unyielding belief that if we only had a

government as responsible as all of you, as compassionate as the American people, that there is no obstacle that we can't overcome. There is no destiny that we cannot fulfill.

Virginia, I have just one word for you, just one word. Tomorrow. Tomorrow. After decades of broken politics in Washington, 8 years of failed policies from George Bush, twenty-one months of campaigning, we are less then one day away from bringing about change in America.

Tomorrow you can turn the page on policies that put greed and irresponsibility before hard work and sacrifice. Tomorrow you can choose policies that invest in our middle class, create new jobs and grow this economy so that everybody has a chance to succeed. Not just the CEO but the secretary and the janitor; not just the factory owner but the men and women who work the factory floor. Tomorrow you can put an end to the politics that would divide a nation just to win an election; that puts reason against reason, and city against town, Republican against Democrat; that asks us to fear at a time when we need to hope.

Tomorrow, at this defining moment in history, you can give this country the change that we need. It starts here in Virginia. It starts here in Manassas. This is where change begins.

Our campaign has not been perfect. There are times when I look back and I've said, "you know I wouldn't have done that if I had thought about it a little bit more." But I'll tell you what. When you think about this campaign we've got a lot to be proud of when it comes to the tone that we have set.

We tried to argue issues and not engage in personal attacks. We've been fierce in defending ourselves but we've tried to make sure that we are always reminding our supporters that all of us are in this together. Black, white, Hispanic, native American, Asian, Democrats and Republicans, young and old, rich and poor, gay and straight, disabled and not disabled, all of us have something to contribute.

We tried to communicate for these last two years that we can't afford the same political games, the same tactics that pit us against one another, that make us afraid of each other. We can't afford that anymore. Not this time. Despite what our opponents might claim, there are no real or fake parts of Virginia anymore and then there are real or fake parts of America. There is no city or town that is more pro-America than anywhere else. We are all one nation. All of us proud. All of us patriots. All of us salute this flag.

The men and women who serve on our battlefields come from many walks of life, different political parties, but they fought together and they bled together. Some die together under the same proud flag. They have not served red America or blue America, they have served the United States of America. And that is what this campaign has been about, we're calling us to serve the United States of America.

In this campaign I have had the privilege to witness what is best in America, in the stories, in the faces, of men and women I have met at countless rallies, town hall meetings, VFW halls, living rooms, diners, all across America, men and women who shared with me their stories and spoke of their struggles but they also spoke of their hopes and dreams. They want for their children a sense of obligation and debts to be paid to earlier generations.

I met one of those women in Greenwood, South Carolina. It was back early when we were way back in the polls. Nobody gave us much of a chance back then. I had gone to South Carolina early in the campaign to see what I could stir up in the way of endorsements, and I was at a legislative dinner sitting next to a state representative that I really wanted to endorse me. So I turned to her and I said "I really want your endorsement." And she looked at me and she said "I'll tell you what, Obama, I will give you my endorsement if you come to my hometown of Greenwood, South Carolina." I must have had a sip of wine or something that night because right away I said "Okay. I'm coming."

So the next time I come to South Carolina it's about a month later. We fly in about midnight. We get to the hotel about one o'clock in the morning. I'm exhausted. I'm dragging my bags to my room when I get a tap on my shoulder and I look back and it is one of my staff people who says "Senator we need to be out of the hotel by 6 a.m." I say "Why is that?" He says "because we have to go to Greenwood, like you promised."

So the next morning I wake up and I feel terrible, and I think I am coming down with a cold, my back is sore, I feel worse than when I went to bed. I open up the curtains in the hotel room to get some sunlight in and hopefully wake me up, but it's pouring down rain. I go outside my room and get the New York Times, and there is a bad story about me in the New York Times. I go downstairs after I pack, and my umbrella blows open and I get soaked, so by the time I get in the car I am mad, I am wet and I am sleepy.

We drive, and we drive, and we drive. It turns out that Greenwood is about an hour and a half from everywhere else. Finally we get to Greenwood.

First of all you do not know you're in Greenwood when you get to Greenwood, there aren't a lot of tall buildings in Greenwood. We pull off to a small building — a little field house in a park — and we go inside, and low and behold, after an hour and a half drive, turns out there are 20 people there. Twenty people. They look all kind of damp and sleepy, maybe they aren't really excited to be there either.

But I am a professional, I've got to do what I got to do. I'm going around, I'm shaking hands, I am saying "How are you doing? What are you doing?"

As I go around the room suddenly I hear this voice cry out behind me "fired up." I'm shocked. I jumped up. I don't know what is going on. But everyone else acts as though this were normal and they say "fired up." Then I hear this voice say "ready to go." And the 20 people in the room act like this happens all the time and they say "ready to go". I don't know what's going on so I looked behind me and there is this small woman, about 60 years old, a little over 5 feet, looks like she just came from church — she's got on a big church hat. She's standing there, she looks at me and she smiles and she says "fired up."

It turns out that she was a city Councilwoman from Greenwood who also moonlights as a private detective. I'm not making this up. And it turns out that she is famous for her chant. She does this where ever she goes. She says "fired up" and the people say "fired up", and she says "ready to go" and they say "ready to go." For the next five minutes she proceeds to do this. "Fired up?" and everyone says "fired up" and she says "ready to go" and they say "ready to go." I'm standing there and I'm thinking I'm being outflanked by this woman. She's stealing my thunder. I look at my staff and they shrugged their shoulders, they don't know how long this is going to go on.

But here's the thing, Virginia. After a minute or so I am feeling kind of fired up. I'm feeling like I'm ready to go. So I join in the chant. It feels good. For the rest of the day, even after we left Greenwood, even though it was still raining, even though I was still not getting big crowds anywhere, even though we hadn't gotten the endorsement from the people we were hoping for, somehow I felt a little lighter, a little better. I'd see my staff and I would say "Are you fired up? and they would say "We are fired up, boss, are you ready to go?" And I'd say "I'm ready to go."

Here's my point, Virginia. That's how this thing started. It shows you what one voice can do. That one voice can change a room. And if a voice can change a room, it can change a city, and if it can change a city, it can change a state, and if it can change a state, it can change a nation, and if it can change a nation, it can change the world.

Virginia, your voice can change the world tomorrow. In 21

hours if you are willing to endure some rain, if you are willing to drag that person you know who is not going to vote, to the polls. If you are willing to organize and volunteer in the offices, if you are willing to stand with me, if you are willing to fight with me, I know your voice will matter.

So I have just one question for you Virginia, Are you fired up? Ready to go? Fired up. Ready to go. Fired up. Ready to go. Fired up. Ready to go.

Virginia, let's go change the world. God bless you and God bless the United States of America.

Election Night Victory Speech
Grant Park, Illinois
November 4, 2008

If there is anyone out there who still doubts that America is a place where all things are possible; who still wonders if the dream of our founders is alive in our time; who still questions the power of our democracy, tonight is your answer.

It's the answer told by lines that stretched around schools and churches in numbers this nation has never seen; by people who waited three hours and four hours, many for the very first time in their lives, because they believed that this time must be different; that their voice could be that difference.

It's the answer spoken by young and old, rich and poor, Democrat and Republican, black, white, Latino, Asian, Native American, gay, straight, disabled and not disabled – Americans who sent a message to the world that we have never been a collection of Red States and Blue States: we are, and always will be, the United States of America.

It's the answer that led those who have been told for so long by so many to be cynical, and fearful, and doubtful of what we can achieve to put their hands on the arc of history and bend it once more toward the hope of a better day.

It's been a long time coming, but tonight, because of what we did on this day, in this election, at this defining moment, change has come to America.

I just received a very gracious call from Senator McCain. He fought long and hard in this campaign, and he's fought even longer and harder for the country he loves. He has endured sacrifices for America that most of us cannot begin to imagine, and we are better off for the service rendered by this brave and selfless leader. I congratulate him and Governor Palin for all they have achieved, and I look forward to working with them to renew this nation's promise in the months ahead.

I want to thank my partner in this journey, a man who campaigned from his heart and spoke for the men and women he grew up with on the streets of Scranton and rode with on that train home to Delaware, the Vice President-elect of the United States, Joe Biden.

I would not be standing here tonight without the unyielding support of my best friend for the last sixteen years, the rock of our family and the love of my life, our nation's next First Lady, Michelle Obama. Sasha and Malia, I love you both so much, and you have earned the new puppy that's coming with us to the White House. And while she's no longer with us, I know my grandmother is watching, along with the family that made me who I am. I miss them tonight, and know that my debt to them is beyond measure.

To my campaign manager David Plouffe, my chief strategist David Axelrod, and the best campaign team ever assembled in the history of politics – you made this happen, and I am forever grateful for what you've sacrificed to get it done.

But above all, I will never forget who this victory truly belongs to – it belongs to you.

I was never the likeliest candidate for this office. We didn't start with much money or many endorsements. Our campaign was not hatched in the halls of Washington – it began in the backyards of Des Moines and the living rooms of Concord and the front porches of Charleston.

It was built by working men and women who dug into what little savings they had to give five dollars and ten dollars and twenty dollars to this cause. It grew strength from the young people who rejected the myth of their generation's apathy; who left their homes and their families for jobs that offered little pay and less sleep; from the not-so-young people who braved the bitter cold and scorching heat to knock on the doors of perfect strangers; from the millions of Americans who volunteered, and organized, and proved that more than two centuries later, a government of the people, by the people and for the people has not perished from this Earth. This is your victory. I know you didn't do this just to win an election and I know you didn't do it for me. You did it because you understand the enormity of the task that lies ahead. For even as we celebrate tonight, we know the challenges that tomorrow will bring are the greatest of our lifetime – two wars, a planet in peril, the worst financial crisis in a century. Even as we stand here tonight, we know there are brave Americans waking up in the deserts of Iraq and the mountains of Afghanistan to risk their lives for us. There are mothers and fathers who will lie awake after their children fall asleep and wonder how they'll make the mortgage, or pay their doctor's bills, or save enough for college. There is new energy to harness and new jobs to be created; new schools to build and threats to meet and alliances to repair.

The road ahead will be long. Our climb will be steep. We may not get there in one year or even one term, but America – I have never been more hopeful than I am tonight that we will get there. I promise you – we as a people will get there.

There will be setbacks and false starts. There are many who won't agree with every decision or policy I make as President, and we know that government can't solve every problem. But I will always be honest with you about the challenges we face. I will listen to you, especially when we disagree. And above all, I will ask you join in the work of remaking this nation the only way it's been done in America for two-hundred and twenty-one years – block by block, brick by brick, calloused hand by calloused hand.

What began twenty-one months ago in the depths of winter must not end on this autumn night. This victory alone is not the change we seek – it is only the chance for us to make that change. And that cannot happen if we go back to the way things were. It cannot happen without you.

So let us summon a new spirit of patriotism; of service and responsibility where each of us resolves to pitch in and work harder and look after not only ourselves, but each other. Let us remember that if this financial crisis taught us anything, it's that we cannot have a thriving Wall Street while Main Street suffers – in this country, we rise or fall as one nation; as one people.

Let us resist the temptation to fall back on the same partisanship and pettiness and immaturity that has poisoned our politics for so long. Let us remember that it was a man from this state who first carried the banner of the Republican Party to the White House – a party founded on the values of self-reliance, individual liberty, and national unity. Those are values we all share, and while the Democratic Party has won a great victory tonight, we do so with a measure of humility and determination to heal the divides that have held back our progress. As Lincoln said to a nation far more divided than ours, "We are not enemies, but friends...though passion may have strained it must not break our bonds of affection." And to those Americans whose support I have yet to earn – I may not have won your vote, but I hear your voices, I need your help, and I will be your President too.

And to all those watching tonight from beyond our shores, from parliaments and palaces to those who are huddled around radios in the forgotten corners of our world – our stories are singular, but our destiny is shared, and a new dawn of American leadership is at hand. To those who would tear this world down – we will defeat you. To those who seek peace and security – we support you. And to all those who have wondered if America's beacon still burns as bright – tonight we proved once more that the true strength of our nation comes not from our the might of our arms or the scale of our wealth, but from the enduring power of our ideals: democracy, liberty, opportunity, and unyielding hope.

For that is the true genius of America – that America can change. Our union can be perfected. And what we have already achieved gives us hope for what we can and must achieve tomorrow.

This election had many firsts and many stories that will be told for generations. But one that's on my mind tonight is about a woman who cast her ballot in Atlanta. She's a lot like the millions of others who stood in line to make their voice heard in this election except for one thing – Ann Nixon Cooper is 106 years old.

She was born just a generation past slavery; a time when there were no cars on the road or planes in the sky; when someone like her couldn't vote for two reasons – because she was a woman and because of the color of her skin.

And tonight, I think about all that she's seen throughout her century in America – the heartache and the hope; the struggle and the progress; the times we were told that we can't, and the people who pressed on with that American creed: Yes we can.

At a time when women's voices were silenced and their hopes dismissed, she lived to see them stand up and speak out and reach for the ballot. Yes we can.

When there was despair in the dust bowl and depression across the land, she saw a nation conquer fear itself with a New Deal, new jobs and a new sense of common purpose. Yes we can.

When the bombs fell on our harbor and tyranny threatened the world, she was there to witness a generation rise to greatness and a democracy was saved. Yes we can.

She was there for the buses in Montgomery, the hoses in Birmingham, a bridge in Selma, and a preacher from Atlanta who told a people that "We Shall Overcome." Yes we can.

A man touched down on the moon, a wall came down in Berlin, a world was connected by our own science and imagination. And this year, in this election, she touched her finger to a screen, and cast her vote, because after 106 years in America, through the best of times and the darkest of hours, she knows how America can change. Yes we can.

America, we have come so far. We have seen so much. But there is so much more to do. So tonight, let us ask ourselves – if our children should live to see the next century; if my daughters should be so lucky to live as long as Ann Nixon Cooper, what change will they see? What progress will we have made?

This is our chance to answer that call. This is our moment. This is our time – to put our people back to work and open doors of opportunity for our kids; to restore prosperity and promote the cause of peace; to reclaim the American Dream and reaffirm that fundamental truth – that out of many, we are one; that while we breathe, we hope, and where we are met with cynicism, and doubt, and those who tell us that we can't, we will respond with that timeless creed that sums up the spirit of a people:

Yes We Can. Thank you, God bless you, and may God Bless the United States of America.

President-elect Barack Obama's
First Weekly Address to the Nation
November 15, 2008

Today, the leaders of the G-20 countries -- a group that includes the world's largest economies -- are gathering in Washington to seek solutions to the ongoing turmoil in our financial markets. I'm glad President Bush has initiated this process -- because our global economic crisis requires a coordinated global response.

And yet, as we act in concert with other nations, we must also act immediately here at home to address America's own economic crisis. This week, amid continued volatility in our markets, we learned that unemployment insurance claims rose to their highest levels since September 11, 2001. We've lost jobs for ten straight months -- nearly 1.2 million jobs this year, many of them in our struggling auto industry. And millions of our fellow citizens lie awake each night wondering how they're going to pay their bills, stay in their homes, and save for retirement.

Make no mistake: this is the greatest economic challenge of our time. And while the road ahead will be long, and the work will be hard, I know that we can steer ourselves out of this crisis -- because here in America we always rise to the moment, no matter how hard. And I am more hopeful than ever before that America will rise once again.

But we must act right now. Next week, Congress will meet to address the spreading impact of the economic crisis. I urge them to pass at least a down-payment on a rescue plan that will create jobs, relieve the squeeze on families, and help get the economy growing again. In particular, we cannot afford to delay providing help for the more than one million Americans who will have exhausted their unemployment insurance by the end of this year. If Congress does not pass an immediate plan that gives the economy the boost it needs, I will make it my first order of business as President.

Even as we dig ourselves out of this recession, we must also recognize that out of this economic crisis comes an opportunity to create new jobs, strengthen our middle class, and keep our economy competitive in the 21st century.

That starts with the kinds of long-term investments that we've neglected for too long. That means putting two million Americans to work rebuilding our crumbling roads, bridges, and schools. It means investing $150 billion to build an American green energy economy that will create five million new jobs, while freeing our nation from the tyranny of foreign oil, and saving our planet for our children. It means making health care affordable for anyone who has it, accessible for anyone who wants it, and reducing costs for small businesses. And it also means giving every child the world-class education they need to compete with any worker, anywhere in the world.

Doing all this will require not just new policies, but a new spirit of service and sacrifice, where each of us resolves to pitch in and work harder and look after not only ourselves, but each other. If this financial crisis has taught us anything, it's that we cannot have a thriving Wall Street while Main Street suffers -- in this country, we rise or fall as one nation; as one people. And that is how we will meet the challenges of our time -- together. Thank you.

President-Elect Barack Obama
Thanksgiving Address to the Nation
Thursday, November 27th, 2008

Nearly 150 years ago, in one of the darkest years of our nation's history, President Abraham Lincoln set aside the last Thursday in November as a day of Thanksgiving. America was split by Civil War. But Lincoln said in his first Thanksgiving decree that difficult times made it even more appropriate for our blessings to be -- and I quote -- "gratefully acknowledged as with one heart and one voice by the whole American people."

This week, the American people came together with family and friends to carry on this distinctly American tradition. We gave thanks for loved ones and for our lasting pride in our communities and our country. We took comfort in good memories while looking forward to the promise of change.

But this Thanksgiving also takes place at a time of great trial for our people.

Across the country, there were empty seats at the table, as brave Americans continue to serve in harm's way from the mountains of Afghanistan to the deserts of Iraq. We honor and give thanks for their sacrifice, and stand by the families who endure their absence with such dignity and resolve.

At home, we face an economic crisis of historic proportions. More and more Americans are worried about losing a job or making their mortgage payment. Workers are wondering if next month's paycheck will pay next month's bills. Retirees are watching their savings disappear, and students are struggling with the cost of tuition.

It's going to take bold and immediate action to confront this crisis. That's why I'm committed to forging a new beginning from the moment I take office as President of the United States. Earlier this week, I announced my economic team. This talented and dedicated group is already hard at work crafting an Economic Recovery Plan that will create or save 2.5 million new jobs, while making the investments we need to fuel long-term economic growth and stability.

But this Thanksgiving, we are reminded that the renewal of our economy won't come from policies and plans alone -- it will take the hard work, innovation, service, and strength of the American people.

I have seen this strength firsthand over many months -- in workers who are ready to power new industries, and farmers and scientists who can tap new sources of energy; in teachers who stay late after school, and parents who put in that extra hour reading to their kids; in young Americans enlisting in a time of war, seniors who volunteer their time, and service programs that bring hope to the hopeless.

It is a testament to our national character that so many Americans took time out this Thanksgiving to help feed the hungry and care for the needy. On Wednesday, I visited a food bank at Saint Columbanus Parish in Chicago. There -- as in so many communities across America -- folks pitched in time and resources to give a lift to their neighbors in need. It is this spirit that binds us together as one

American family -- the belief that we rise and fall as one people; that we want that American Dream not just for ourselves, but for each other.

That's the spirit we must summon as we make a new beginning for our nation. Times are tough. There are difficult months ahead. But we can renew our nation the same way that we have in the many years since Lincoln's first Thanksgiving: by coming together to overcome adversity; by reaching for -- and working for -- new horizons of opportunity for all Americans.

So this weekend -- with one heart, and one voice, the American people can give thanks that a new and brighter day is yet to come.

President-Elect Barack Obama
Weekly Address
Saturday, December 6, 2008

Yesterday, we received another painful reminder of the serious economic challenge our country is facing when we learned that 533,000 jobs were lost in November alone, the single worst month of job loss in over three decades. That puts the total number of jobs lost in this recession at nearly 2 million.

But this isn't about numbers. It's about each of the families those numbers represent. It's about the rising unease and frustration that so many of you are feeling during this holiday season. Will you be able to put your kids through college? Will you be able to afford health care? Will you be able to retire with dignity and security? Will your job or your husband's job or your daughter's or son's job be the next one cut?

These are the questions that keep so many Americans awake at night. But it is not the first time these questions have been asked. We have faced difficult times before, times when our economic destiny seemed to be slipping out of our hands. And at each moment, we have risen to meet the challenge, as one people united by a sense of common purpose. And I know that Americans can rise to the moment once again.

But we need action – and action now. That is why I have asked my economic team to develop an economic recovery plan for both Wall Street and Main Street that will help save or create at least two and a half million jobs, while rebuilding our infrastructure, improving our schools, reducing our dependence on oil, and saving billions of dollars.

We won't do it the old Washington way. We won't just throw money at the problem. We'll measure progress by the reforms we make and the results we achieve -- by the jobs we create, by the energy we save, by whether America is more competitive in the world.

Today, I am announcing a few key parts of my plan. First, we will launch a massive effort to make public buildings more energy-efficient. Our government now pays the highest energy bill in the world. We need to change that. We need to upgrade our federal buildings by replacing old heating systems and installing efficient light bulbs. That won't just save you, the American taxpayer, billions of dollars each year. It will put people back to work.

Second, we will create millions of jobs by making the single largest new investment in our national infrastructure since the creation of the federal highway system in the 1950s. We'll invest your precious tax dollars in new and smarter ways, and we'll set a simple rule – use it or lose it. If a state doesn't act quickly to invest in roads and bridges in their communities, they'll lose the money.

Third, my economic recovery plan will launch the most sweeping effort to modernize and upgrade school buildings that this country has ever seen. We will repair broken schools, make them energy-efficient, and put new computers in our classrooms. Because to help our children compete in a 21st century economy, we need to send them to 21st century schools.

As we renew our schools and highways, we'll also renew our information superhighway. It is unacceptable that the United States ranks 15th in the world in broadband adoption. Here, in the country that invented the internet, every child should have the chance to get online, and they'll get that chance when I'm President – because that's how we'll strengthen America's competitiveness in the world.

In addition to connecting our libraries and schools to the internet, we must also ensure that our hospitals are connected to each other through the internet. That is why the economic recovery plan I'm proposing will help modernize our health care system – and that won't just save jobs, it will save lives. We will make sure that every doctor's office and hospital in this country is using cutting edge technology and electronic medical records so that we can cut red tape, prevent medical mistakes, and help save billions of dollars each year.

These are a few parts of the economic recovery plan that I will be rolling out in the coming weeks. When Congress reconvenes, I look forward to working with them to pass a plan immediately. We need to act with the urgency this moment demands to save or create at least 2.5 million jobs so that the nearly two million Americans who've lost them know that they have a future. And that's exactly what I intend to do as President of the United States.

President-elect Barack Obama
Address on the Economy
Saturday, December 13, 2008

Earlier this week, we learned that the number of Americans filing their first claim for unemployment insurance rose to a nearly 30-year high. This news reflects the pain that's been rippling across our entire economy. Jobs are being cut. Wages are being slashed. Credit is tight and people can't get loans. In cities and towns all across this country, families enter a holiday season with unease and uncertainty.

To end this economic crisis, we must end the mortgage crisis where it began. This all started when Americans took out mortgages they couldn't afford. Some were reckless, aware of the risks they were accepting, but many were innocent, tricked by lenders out to make a quick buck. With banks creating securities they could not value, and regulators looking the other way, the problem began infecting the whole economy, leading to the crisis we're now facing.

One in ten families who owns a home is now in some form of distress, the most ever recorded. This is deeply troubling. It not only shakes the foundation of our economy, but the foundation of the American Dream. There is nothing more fundamental than having a home to call your own. It's not just a place to live or raise your children or return after a hard day's work -- it's the cornerstone of a family's financial security.

To stem the rising tide of foreclosures and strengthen our

economy, I've asked my economic team to develop a bold plan that will dramatically increase the number of families who can stay in their homes. But this plan will only work with a comprehensive, coordinated federal effort to make it a reality. We need every part of our government working together -- from the Treasury Department to the Federal Deposit Insurance Corporation, the agency that protects the money you've put in the bank. And few will be more essential to this effort than the Department of Housing and Urban Development.

From providing shelter to those displaced by Katrina to giving help to those facing the loss of a home to revitalizing our cities and communities, HUD's role has never been more important. Since its founding, HUD has been dedicated to tearing down barriers in access to affordable housing -- in an effort to make America more equal and more just. Too often, these efforts have had mixed results.

That is why we cannot keep doing things the old Washington way. We cannot keep throwing money at the problem, hoping for a different result. We need to approach the old challenge of affordable housing with new energy, new ideas, and a new, efficient style of leadership. We need to understand that the old ways of looking at our cities just won't do. That means promoting cities as the backbone of regional growth by not only solving the problems in our cities, but seizing the opportunities in our growing suburbs, exurbs, and metropolitan areas. No one knows this better than the outstanding public servant I am announcing today as our next Secretary of

Housing and Urban Development -- Shaun Donovan.

As Commissioner of Housing Preservation and Development in New York City, Shaun has led the effort to create the largest housing plan in the nation, helping hundreds of thousands of our citizens buy or rent their homes. Prior to joining Mayor Bloomberg's administration, Shaun worked both in business, where he was responsible for affordable housing investments, and at one of our nation's top universities, where he researched and wrote about housing issues. This appointment represents something of a homecoming for Shaun, who worked at HUD in the Clinton administration, leading an effort to help make housing affordable for nearly two million Americans. Trained as an architect, Shaun understands housing down to how homes are designed, built, and wired.

With experience that stretches from the public sector to the private sector to academia, Shaun will bring to this important post fresh thinking, unencumbered by old ideology and outdated ideas. He understands that we need to move past the stale arguments that say low-income Americans shouldn't even try to own a home or that our mortgage crisis is due solely to a few greedy lenders. He knows that we can put the dream of owning a home within reach for more families, so long as we're making loans in the right way, and so long as those who buy a home are prepared for the responsibilities of homeownership.

In the end, expanding access to affordable housing isn't just about caring for the least fortunate among us and strengthening our middle class -- it's about ending our housing mess, climbing out of our financial crisis, and putting our economy on the path to long-term growth and prosperity. And that is what Shaun and I will work to do together when I am President of the United States.

Thank you.

President-Elect Barack Obama
Holiday Address to the Nation
December 27, 2008

This week, Americans are gathering with family and friends across the country to celebrate the blessings of Christmas and the holiday season.

As we celebrate this joyous time of year, our thoughts turn to the brave men and women who serve our country far from home. Their extraordinary and selfless sacrifice is an inspiration to us all, and part of the unbroken line of heroism that has made our freedom and prosperity possible for over two centuries.

Many troops are serving their second, third, or fourth tour of duty. And we are reminded that they are more than dedicated Soldiers, Sailors, Airmen, Marines and Coast Guard – they are devoted fathers and mothers; husbands and wives; sons and daughters; and sisters and brothers.

This holiday season, their families celebrate with a joy that is muted knowing that a loved one is absent, and sometimes in danger. In towns and cities across America, there is an empty seat at the dinner table; in distant bases and on ships at sea, our servicemen and women can only wonder at the look on their child's face as they open a gift back home.

Our troops and military families have won the respect and gratitude of their broader American family. Michelle and I have them in our prayers this Christmas, and we must all continue to offer them our full support in the weeks and months to come. .

These are also tough times for many Americans struggling in our sluggish economy. As we count the higher blessings of faith and family, we know that millions of Americans don't have a job. Many more are struggling to pay the bills or stay in their homes. From students to seniors, the future seems uncertain.

That is why this season of giving should also be a time to renew a sense of common purpose and shared citizenship. Now, more than ever, we must rededicate ourselves to the notion that we share a common destiny as Americans – that I am my brother's keeper, I am my sister's keeper. Now, we must all do our part to serve one another; to seek new ideas and new innovation; and to start a new chapter for our great country.

That is the spirit that will guide my Administration in the New Year. If the American people come together and put their shoulder to the wheel of history, then I know that we can put our people back to work and point our country in a new direction. That is how we will see ourselves through this time of crisis, and reach the promise of a brighter day.

After all, that is what Americans have always done.

232 years ago, when America was newly born as a nation, George Washington and his Army faced impossible odds as they struggled to free themselves from the grip of an empire.

It was Christmas Day -- December 25th, 1776 – that they fought through ice and cold to make an improbable crossing of the Delaware

River. They caught the enemy off guard, won victories in Trenton and Princeton, and gave new momentum to a beleaguered Army and new hope to the cause of Independence.

Many ages have passed since that first American Christmas. We have crossed many rivers as a people. But the lessons that have carried us through are the same lessons that we celebrate every Christmas season -- the same lessons that guide us to this very day: that hope endures, and that a new birth of peace is always possible.

President-Elect Barack Obama
American Recovery and Reinvestment
George Mason University
January 8, 2009

Throughout America's history, there have been some years that simply rolled into the next without much notice or fanfare. Then there are the years that come along once in a generation – the kind that mark a clean break from a troubled past, and set a new course for our nation.

This is one of those years.

We start 2009 in the midst of a crisis unlike any we have seen in our lifetime – a crisis that has only deepened over the last few weeks. Nearly two million jobs have now been lost, and on Friday we are likely to learn that we lost more jobs last year than at any time since World War II. Just in the past year, another 2.8 million Americans who want and need full-time work have had to settle for part-time jobs. Manufacturing has hit a twenty-eight year low. Many businesses cannot borrow or make payroll. Many families cannot pay their bills or their mortgage. Many workers are watching their life savings disappear. And many, many Americans are both anxious and uncertain of what the future will hold.

I don't believe it's too late to change course, but it will be if we don't take dramatic action as soon as possible. If nothing is done, this recession could linger for years. The unemployment rate could reach double digits. Our economy could fall $1 trillion short of its full capacity, which translates into more than $12,000 in lost income for a family of four. We could lose a generation of potential and promise, as more young Americans are forced to forgo dreams of college or the chance to train for the jobs of the future. And our nation could lose the competitive edge that has served as a foundation for our strength and standing in the world.

In short, a bad situation could become dramatically worse.

This crisis did not happen solely by some accident of history or normal turn of the business cycle, and we won't get out of it by simply waiting for a better day to come, or relying on the worn-out dogmas of the past. We arrived at this point due to an era of profound irresponsibility that stretched from corporate boardrooms to the halls of power in Washington, DC. For years, too many Wall Street executives made imprudent and dangerous decisions, seeking profits with too little regard for risk, too little regulatory scrutiny, and too little accountability. Banks made loans without concern for whether borrowers could repay them, and some borrowers took advantage of cheap credit to take on debt they couldn't afford. Politicians spent taxpayer money without wisdom or discipline, and too often focused on scoring political points instead of the problems they were sent here to solve. The result has been a devastating loss of trust and confidence in our economy, our financial markets, and our government.

Now, the very fact that this crisis is largely of our own making means that it is not beyond our ability to solve. Our problems are rooted in past mistakes, not our capacity for future greatness. It will take time, perhaps many years, but we can rebuild that lost trust and confidence. We can restore opportunity and prosperity. We should never forget that our workers are still more productive than any on Earth. Our universities are still the envy of the world. We are still home to the most brilliant minds, the most creative entrepreneurs, and the most advanced technology and innovation that history has ever known. And we are still the nation that has overcome great fears and improbable odds. If we act with the urgency and seriousness that this moment requires, I know that we can do it again.

That is why I have moved quickly to work with my economic team and leaders of both parties on an American Recovery and Reinvestment Plan that will immediately jumpstart job creation and long-term growth.

It's a plan that represents not just new policy, but a whole new approach to meeting our most urgent challenges. For if we hope to end this crisis, we must end the culture of anything goes that helped create it – and this change must begin in Washington. It is time to trade old habits for a new spirit of responsibility. It is time to finally change the ways of Washington so that we can set a new and better course for America.

There is no doubt that the cost of this plan will be considerable. It will certainly add to the budget deficit in the short-term. But equally certain are the consequences of doing too little or nothing at all, for that will lead to an even greater deficit of jobs, incomes, and confidence in our economy. It is true that we cannot depend on government alone to create jobs or long-term growth, but at this particular moment, only government can provide the short-term boost necessary to lift us from a recession this deep and severe. Only government can break the vicious cycles that are crippling our economy – where a lack of spending leads to lost jobs which leads to even less spending; where an inability to lend and borrow stops growth and leads to even less credit.

That is why we need to act boldly and act now to reverse these cycles. That's why we need to put money in the pockets of the American people, create new jobs, and invest in our future. That's why we need to re-start the flow of credit and restore the rules of the road that will ensure a crisis like this never happens again.

That work begins with this plan – a plan I am confident will save or create at least three million jobs over the next few years. It is not just another public works program. It's a plan that recognizes both the paradox and the promise of this moment – the fact that there are millions of Americans trying to find work, even as, all around the country, there is so much work to be done. That's why we'll invest in priorities like energy and education; health care and a new infrastructure that are necessary to keep us strong and competitive in the 21st century. That's why the overwhelming majority of the jobs created will be in the private sector, while our plan will save the public sector jobs of teachers, cops, firefighters and others who provide vital services.

To finally spark the creation of a clean energy economy, we will double the production of alternative energy in the next three years. We will modernize more than 75% of federal buildings and improve the energy efficiency of two million American homes, saving consumers and taxpayers billions on our energy bills. In the process, we will put Americans to work in new jobs that pay well and can't be outsourced – jobs building solar panels and wind turbines; constructing fuel-efficient cars and buildings; and developing the new energy technologies that will lead to even more jobs, more savings, and a cleaner, safer planet in the bargain.

To improve the quality of our health care while lowering its cost, we will make the immediate investments necessary to ensure that within five years, all of America's medical records are computerized. This will cut waste, eliminate red tape, and reduce the need to repeat expensive medical tests. But it just won't save billions of dollars and thousands of jobs – it will save lives by reducing the deadly but preventable medical errors that pervade our health care system.

To give our children the chance to live out their dreams in a world that's never been more competitive, we will equip tens of thousands of schools, community colleges, and public universities with 21st century classrooms, labs, and libraries. We'll provide new computers, new technology, and new training for teachers so that students in Chicago and Boston can compete with kids in Beijing for the high-tech, high-wage jobs of the future.

To build an economy that can lead this future, we will begin to rebuild America. Yes, we'll put people to work repairing crumbling roads, bridges, and schools by eliminating the backlog of well-planned, worthy and needed infrastructure projects. But we'll also do more to retrofit America for a global economy. That means updating the way we get our electricity by starting to build a new smart grid that will save us money, protect our power sources from blackout or attack, and deliver clean, alternative forms of energy to every corner of our nation. It means expanding broadband lines across America, so that a small business in a rural town can connect and compete with their counterparts anywhere in the world. And it means investing in the science, research, and technology that will lead to new medical breakthroughs, new discoveries, and entire new industries.

Finally, this recovery and reinvestment plan will provide immediate relief to states, workers, and families who are bearing the brunt of this recession. To get people spending again, 95% of working families will receive a $1,000 tax cut – the first stage of a middle-class tax cut that I promised during the campaign and will include in our next budget. To help Americans who have lost their jobs and can't find new ones, we'll continue the bipartisan extensions of unemployment insurance and health care coverage to help them through this crisis. Government at every level will have to tighten its belt, but we'll help struggling states avoid harmful budget cuts, as long as they take responsibility and use the money to maintain essential services like police, fire, education, and health care.

I understand that some might be skeptical of this plan. Our government has already spent a good deal of money, but we haven't yet seen that translate into more jobs or higher incomes or renewed confidence in our economy. That's why the American Recovery and Reinvestment Plan won't just throw money at our problems – we'll invest in what works. The true test of the policies we'll pursue won't be whether they're Democratic or Republican ideas, but whether they create jobs, grow our economy, and put the American Dream within reach of the American people.

Instead of politicians doling out money behind a veil of secrecy, decisions about where we invest will be made transparently, and informed by independent experts wherever possible. Every American will be able to hold Washington accountable for these decisions by going online to see how and where their tax dollars are being spent. And as I announced yesterday, we will launch an unprecedented effort to eliminate unwise and unnecessary spending that has never been more unaffordable for our nation and our children's future than it is right now.

We have to make tough choices and smart investments today so that as the economy recovers, the deficit starts to come down. We cannot have a solid recovery if our people and our businesses don't have confidence that we're getting our fiscal house in order. That's why our goal is not to create a slew of new government programs, but a foundation for long-term economic growth.

That also means an economic recovery plan that is free from earmarks and pet projects. I understand that every member of Congress has ideas on how to spend money. Many of these projects are worthy, and benefit local communities. But this emergency legislation must not be the vehicle for those aspirations. This must be a time when leaders in both parties put the urgent needs of our nation above our own narrow interests.

Now, this recovery plan alone will not solve all the problems that led us into this crisis. We must also work with the same sense of urgency to stabilize and repair the financial system we all depend on. That means using our full arsenal of tools to get credit flowing again to families and business, while restoring confidence in our markets. It means launching a sweeping effort to address the foreclosure crisis so that we can keep responsible families in their homes. It means preventing the catastrophic failure of financial institutions whose collapse could endanger the entire economy, but only with maximum protections for taxpayers and a clear understanding that government support for any company is an extraordinary action that must come with significant restrictions on the firms that receive support. And it means reforming a weak and outdated regulatory system so that we can better withstand financial shocks and better protect consumers, investors, and businesses from the reckless greed and risk-taking that must never endanger our prosperity again.

No longer can we allow Wall Street wrongdoers to slip through regulatory cracks. No longer can we allow special interests to put their thumbs on the economic scales. No longer can we allow the unscrupulous lending and borrowing that leads only to destructive cycles of bubble and bust.

It is time to set a new course for this economy, and that change must begin now. We should have an open and honest discussion about this recovery plan in the days ahead, but I urge Congress to move as quickly as possible on behalf of the American people. For every day we wait or point fingers or drag our feet, more Americans will lose their jobs. More families will lose their savings. More dreams will be deferred and denied. And our nation will sink deeper into a crisis that, at some point, we may not be able to reverse.

That is not the country I know, and it is not a future I will accept as President of the United States. A world that depends on the strength of our economy is now watching and waiting for America to lead once more. And that is what we will do.

It will not come easy or happen overnight, and it is altogether likely that things may get worse before they get better. But that is all the more reason for Congress to act without delay. I know the scale of this plan is unprecedented, but so is the severity of our situation. We have already tried the wait-and-see approach to our problems, and it is the same approach that helped lead us to this day of reckoning.

That is why the time has come to build a 21st century economy in which hard work and responsibility are once again rewarded. That's why I'm asking Congress to work with me and my team day and night, on weekends if necessary, to get the plan passed in the next few weeks. That's why I'm calling on all Americans – Democrats and Republicans – to put good ideas ahead of the old ideological battles; a sense of common purpose above the same narrow partisanship; and insist that the first question each of us asks isn't "What's good for me?" but "What's good for the country my children will inherit?"

More than any program or policy, it is this spirit that will enable us to confront this challenge with the same spirit that has led previous generations to face down war, depression, and fear itself. And if we do – if we are able to summon that spirit again; if are able to look out for one another, and listen to one another, and do our part for our nation and for posterity, then I have no doubt that years from now, we will look back on 2009 as one of those years that marked another new and hopeful beginning for the United States of America. Thank you, God Bless You, and may God Bless America.

Weekly Address to the Nation
January 10, 2008
Washington, D.C.

We start this new year in the midst of an economic crisis unlike any we have seen in our lifetime. We learned yesterday that in the past month alone, we lost more than half a million jobs – a total of nearly 2.6 million in the year 2008. Another 3.4 million Americans who want and need full-time work have had to settle for part-time jobs. And families across America are feeling the pinch as they watch debts mount, bills pile up and savings disappear.

These numbers are a stark reminder that we simply cannot continue on our current path. If nothing is done, economists from across the spectrum tell us that this recession could linger for years and the unemployment rate could reach double digits – and they warn that our nation could lose the competitive edge that has served as a foundation for our strength and standing in the world.

It's not too late to change course – but only if we take immediate and dramatic action. Our first job is to put people back to work and get our economy working again. This is an extraordinary challenge, which is why I've taken the extraordinary step of working – even before I take office – with my economic team and leaders of both parties on an American Recovery and Reinvestment Plan that will call for major investments to revive our economy, create jobs, and lay a solid foundation for future growth.

I asked my nominee for Chair of the Council of Economic

Advisers, Dr. Christina Romer, and the Vice President-Elect's Chief Economic Adviser, Dr. Jared Bernstein, to conduct a rigorous analysis of this plan and come up with projections of how many jobs it will create – and what kind of jobs they will be. Today, I am releasing a report of their findings so that the American people can see exactly what this plan will mean for their families, their communities, and our economy.

The report confirms that our plan will likely save or create three to four million jobs. 90 percent of these jobs will be created in the private sector – the remaining 10 percent are mainly public sector jobs we save, like the teachers, police officers, firefighters and others who provide vital services in our communities.

The jobs we create will be in businesses large and small across a wide range of industries. And they'll be the kind of jobs that don't just put people to work in the short term, but position our economy to lead the world in the long-term.

We'll create nearly half a million jobs by investing in clean energy – by committing to double the production of alternative energy in the next three years, and by modernizing more than 75% of federal buildings and improving the energy efficiency of two million American homes. These made-in-America jobs building solar panels and wind turbines, developing fuel-efficient cars and new energy technologies pay well, and they can't be outsourced.

We'll create hundreds of thousands of jobs by improving health care – transitioning to a nationwide system of computerized medical records that won't just save money, but save lives by preventing deadly medical errors. And we'll create hundreds of thousands more jobs in education, equipping tens of thousands of schools with 21st century classrooms, labs and computers to help our kids compete with any worker in the world for any job.

We'll put nearly 400,000 people to work by repairing our infrastructure – our crumbling roads, bridges and schools. And we'll build the new infrastructure we need to succeed in this new century, investing in science and technology, and laying down miles of new broadband l ines so that businesses across our nation can compete with their counterparts around the world.

Finally, we won't just create jobs, we'll also provide help for those who've lost theirs, and for states and families who've been hardest-hit by this recession. That means bi-partisan extensions of unemployment insurance and health care coverage; a $1,000 tax cut for 95 percent of working families; and assistance to help states avoid harmful budget cuts in essential services like police, fire, education and health care.

Now, given the magnitude of the challenges we face, none of this will come easy. Recovery won't happen overnight, and it's likely that things will get worse before they get better.

But we have come through moments like this before. We are the nation that has faced down war, depression and fear itself – each time, refusing to yield; each time, refusing to accept a lesser fate. That is the spirit that has always sustained us – that belief that our destiny is not written for us, but by us; that our success is not a matter of chance, but of our own courage and determination. Our resources may be finite, but our will is infinite. And I am confident that if we come together and summon that great American spirit once again, we will meet the challenges of our time and write the next great chapter in our American story.

Editor's note: Three days before his inauguration, President-Elect Barack Obama started a whistle-stop train trip to Washington D.C. that tracked Abraham Lincoln's historic route to his inauguration. This speech was given shortly before he boarded the train.

A New Declaration of Independence
Philadelphia, Pennsylvania
January 17, 2009

We are here to mark the beginning of our journey to Washington. This is fitting because it was here, in this city, that our American journey began. It was here that a group of farmers and lawyers, merchants and soldiers, gathered to declare their independence and lay claim to a destiny that they were being denied.

It was a risky thing, meeting as they did in that summer of 1776. There was no guarantee that their fragile experiment would find success. More than once in those early years did the odds seem insurmountable. More than once did the fishermen, laborers and craftsmen who called themselves an army face the prospect of defeat.

And yet, they were willing to put all they were and all they had on the line — their lives, their fortunes and their sacred honor — for a set of ideals that continue to light the world. That we are equal. That our rights to life, liberty and the pursuit of happiness come not from our laws, but from our maker. And that a government of, by and for the people can endure. It was these ideals that led us to declare independence and craft our constitution, producing documents that were imperfect but had within them, like our nation itself, the capacity to be made more perfect.

We are here today not simply to pay tribute to our first patriots but to take up the work that they began. The trials we face are very different now, but severe in their own right. Only a handful of times in our history has a generation been confronted with challenges so vast. An economy that is faltering. Two wars, one that needs to be ended responsibly, one that needs to be waged wisely. A planet that is warming from our unsustainable dependence on oil.

And yet while our problems may be new, what is required to overcome them is not. What is required is the same perseverance and idealism that our founders displayed. What is required is a new declaration of independence, not just in our nation, but in our own lives — from ideology and small thinking, prejudice and bigotry — an appeal not to our easy instincts but to our better angels.

That is the reason I launched my campaign for the presidency nearly two years ago. I did so in the belief that the most fundamental American ideal, that a better life is in store for all those willing to work for it, was slipping out of reach. That Washington was serving the interests of the few, not the many. And that our politics had grown too small for the scale of the challenges we faced.

But I also believed something else. I believed that our future is our choice and that if we could just recognize ourselves in one another and bring everyone together — Democrats, Republicans and independents, north, south, east and west, black, white, Latino, Asian and Native American, gay and straight, disabled and not — then not only would we restore hope and opportunity in places that yearned for both, but maybe, just maybe, we might perfect our union in the process.

This is what I believed, but you made this belief real. You proved once more that people who love this country can change it. And as I prepare to leave for Washington on a trip that you made possible, know that I will not be traveling alone. I will be taking with me some of the men and women I met along the way, Americans from every corner of this country, whose hopes and heartaches were the core of our cause; whose dreams and struggles have become my own.

Theirs are the voices I will carry with me every day in the White House. Theirs are the stories I will be thinking of when we deliver the changes you elected me to make. When Americans are returning to work and sleeping easier at night knowing their jobs are secure, I will be thinking of people like Mark Dowell, who's worried his job at Ford will be the next one cut, a devastating prospect with the teenage daughters he has back home.

When affordable health care is no longer something we hope for, but something we can count on, I will be thinking of working moms like Shandra Jackson, who was diagnosed with an illness and is now burdened with higher medical bills on top of child care for her 11-year-old son.

When we are welcoming back our loved ones from a war in Iraq that we've brought to an end, I will be thinking of our brave servicemen and women sacrificing around the world, of veterans like Tony Fischer, who served two tours in Iraq, and all those returning home, unable to find a job.

These are the stories that will drive me in the days ahead. They are different stories, told by men and women whose journeys may seem separate. And yet, what you showed me time and again is that no matter who we are or what we look like, no matter where we come from or what faith we practice, we are a people of common hopes and common dreams, who ask only for what was promised us as Americans — that we might make of our lives what we will and see our children climb higher than we did.

We recognize that such enormous challenges will not be solved quickly. There will be false starts and setbacks, frustrations and disappointments. And we will be called to show patience even as we act with fierce urgency.

But we should never forget that we are the heirs of that first band of patriots, ordinary men and women who refused to give up when it all seemed so improbable; and who somehow believed that they had the power to make the world anew. That is the spirit that we must reclaim today.

For the American Revolution did not end when British guns fell silent. It was never something to be won only on a battlefield or fulfilled only in our founding documents. It was not simply a struggle to break free from empire and declare independence. The American

Revolution was — and remains — an ongoing struggle "in the minds and hearts of the people" to live up to our founding creed.

Starting now, let's take up in our own lives the work of perfecting our union.

Let's build a government that is responsible to the people, and accept our own responsibilities as citizens to hold our government accountable.

Let's all of us do our part to rebuild this country.

Let's make sure this election is not the end of what we do to change America, but the beginning.

Join me in this effort. Join one another in this effort. And together, mindful of our proud history, hopeful for the future, let's seek a better world in our time. Thank you.

Lincoln Memorial Inauguration Celebration
January 18, 2009
Washington D.C.

I want to thank all the speakers and performers for reminding us, through song and through words, just what it is that we love about America. And I want to thank all of you for braving the cold and the crowds and traveling in some cases thousands of miles to join us here today. Welcome to Washington, and welcome to this celebration of American renewal.

In the course of our history, only a handful of generations have been asked to confront challenges as serious as the ones we face right now. Our nation is at war. Our economy is in crisis. Millions of Americans are losing their jobs and their homes; they're worried about how they'll afford college for their kids or pay the stack of bills on their kitchen table. And most of all, they are anxious and uncertain about the future — about whether this generation of Americans will be able to pass on what's best about this country to our children and their children.

I won't pretend that meeting any one of these challenges will be easy. It will take more than a month or a year, and it will likely take many. Along the way there will be setbacks and false starts and days that test our fundamental resolve as a nation.

But despite all of this — despite the enormity of the task that lies ahead -- I stand here today as hopeful as ever that the United States of America will endure, that it will prevail, that the dream of our founders will live on in our time.

What gives me hope is what I see when I look out across this mall. For in these monuments are chiseled those unlikely stories that affirm our unyielding faith -- a faith that anything is possible in America. Rising before us stands a memorial to a man who led a small band of farmers and shopkeepers in revolution against the army of an Empire, all for the sake of an idea.

On the ground below is a tribute to a generation that withstood war and depression -- men and women like my grandparents who toiled on bomber assembly lines and marched across Europe to free the world from tyranny's grasp. Directly in front of us is a pool that still reflects the dream of a King, and the glory of a people who marched and bled so that their children might be judged by their character's content. And behind me, watching over the union he saved, sits the man who in so many ways made this day possible.

And yet, as I stand here today, what gives me the greatest hope of all is not the stone and marble that surrounds us today, but what fills the spaces in between. It is you -- Americans of every race and region and station who came here because you believe in what this country can be and because you want to help us get there.

It is the same thing that gave me hope from the day we began this campaign for the presidency nearly two years ago; a belief that if we could just recognize ourselves in one another and bring everyone together -- Democrats, Republicans, independents; Latino, Asian and Native American; black and white, gay and straight, disabled and not

-- then not only would we restore hope and opportunity in places that yearned for both, but maybe, just maybe, we might perfect our union in the process.

This is what I believed, but you made this belief real. You proved once more that people who love this country can change it. And as I prepare to assume the presidency, yours are the voices I will take with me every day when I walk into that Oval Office -- the voices of men and women who have different stories but hold common hopes; who ask only for what was promised us as Americans -- that we might make of our lives what we will and see our children climb higher than we did.

It is this thread that binds us together in common effort; that runs through every memorial on this mall; that connects us to all those who struggled and sacrificed and stood here before.

It is how this nation has overcome the greatest differences and the longest odds -- because there is no obstacle that can stand in the way of millions of voices calling for change.

That is the belief with which we began this campaign, and that is how we will overcome what ails us now. There is no doubt that our road will be long, that our climb will be steep. But never forget that the true character of our nation is revealed not during times of comfort and ease, but by the right we do when the moment is hard. I ask you to help reveal that character once more, and together, we can carry forward as one nation, and one people, the legacy of our forefathers that we celebrate today.

Thank you, America. God bless you.

President Barack Obama
Inaugural Address
January 20, 2009
Washington, D.C.

My fellow citizens:

I stand here today humbled by the task before us, grateful for the trust you have bestowed, mindful of the sacrifices borne by our ancestors. I thank President Bush for his service to our nation, as well as the generosity and cooperation he has shown throughout this transition.

Forty-four Americans have now taken the presidential oath. The words have been spoken during rising tides of prosperity and the still waters of peace. Yet, every so often the oath is taken amidst gathering clouds and raging storms. At these moments, America has carried on not simply because of the skill or vision of those in high office, but because We the People have remained faithful to the ideals of our forbearers, and true to our founding documents.

So it has been. So it must be with this generation of Americans.

That we are in the midst of crisis is now well understood. Our nation is at war, against a far-reaching network of violence and hatred. Our economy is badly weakened, a consequence of greed and irresponsibility on the part of some, but also our collective failure to make hard choices and prepare the nation for a new age. Homes have been lost; jobs shed; businesses shuttered. Our health care is too costly; our schools fail too many; and each day brings further evidence that the ways we use energy strengthen our adversaries and threaten our planet.

These are the indicators of crisis, subject to data and statistics. Less measurable but no less profound is a sapping of confidence across our land - a nagging fear that America's decline is inevitable, and that the next generation must lower its sights.

Today I say to you that the challenges we face are real. They are serious and they are many. They will not be met easily or in a short span of time. But know this, America - they will be met.

On this day, we gather because we have chosen hope over fear, unity of purpose over conflict and discord.

On this day, we come to proclaim an end to the petty grievances and false promises, the recriminations and worn out dogmas, that for far too long have strangled our politics.

We remain a young nation, but in the words of Scripture, the time has come to set aside childish things. The time has come to reaffirm our enduring spirit; to choose our better history; to carry forward that precious gift, that noble idea, passed on from generation to generation: the God-given promise that all are equal, all are free, and all deserve a chance to pursue their full measure of happiness.

In reaffirming the greatness of our nation, we understand that greatness is never a given. It must be earned. Our journey has never been one of short-cuts or settling for less. It has not been the path for the faint-hearted - for those who prefer leisure over work, or seek only the pleasures of riches and fame. Rather, it has been the risk-takers, the doers, the makers of things - some celebrated but more often men and women obscure in their labor, who have carried us up the long, rugged path towards prosperity and freedom.

For us, they packed up their few worldly possessions and traveled across oceans in search of a new life.

For us, they toiled in sweatshops and settled the West; endured the lash of the whip and plowed the hard earth.

For us, they fought and died, in places like Concord and Gettysburg; Normandy and Khe Sahn.

Time and again these men and women struggled and sacrificed and worked till their hands were raw so that we might live a better life. They saw America as bigger than the sum of our individual ambitions; greater than all the differences of birth or wealth or faction.

This is the journey we continue today. We remain the most prosperous, powerful nation on Earth. Our workers are no less productive than when this crisis began. Our minds are no less inventive, our goods and services no less needed than they were last week or last month or last year. Our capacity remains undiminished. But our time of standing pat, of protecting narrow interests and putting off unpleasant decisions - that time has surely passed. Starting today, we must pick ourselves up, dust ourselves off, and begin again the work of remaking America.

For everywhere we look, there is work to be done. The state of the economy calls for action, bold and swift, and we will act - not only to create new jobs, but to lay a new foundation for growth. We will build the roads and bridges, the electric grids and digital lines that feed our commerce and bind us together. We will restore science to its rightful place, and wield technology's wonders to raise health care's quality and lower its cost. We will harness the sun and the winds and the soil to fuel our cars and run our factories. And we will transform our schools and colleges and universities to meet the demands of a new age. All this we can do. And all this we will do.

Now, there are some who question the scale of our ambitions - who suggest that our system cannot tolerate too many big plans. Their memories are short. For they have forgotten what this country has already done; what free men and women can achieve when imagination is joined to common purpose, and necessity to courage.

What the cynics fail to understand is that the ground has shifted beneath them - that the stale political arguments that have consumed us for so long no longer apply. The question we ask today is not whether our government is too big or too small, but whether it works - whether it helps families find jobs at a decent wage, care they can afford, a retirement that is dignified. Where the answer is yes, we intend to move forward. Where the answer is no, programs will end. And those of us who manage the public's dollars will be held to account - to spend wisely, reform bad habits, and do our business in the light of day - because only then can we restore the vital trust between a people and their government.

Nor is the question before us whether the market is a force for good or ill. Its power to generate wealth and expand freedom is unmatched, but this crisis has reminded us that without a watchful eye, the market can spin out of control - and that a nation cannot prosper long when it favors only the prosperous. The success of our economy has always depended not just on the size of our Gross Domestic Product, but on the reach of our prosperity; on our ability to extend opportunity to every willing heart - not out of charity, but because it is the surest route to our common good.

As for our common defense, we reject as false the choice between our safety and our ideals. Our Founding Fathers, faced with perils we can scarcely imagine, drafted a charter to assure the rule of law and the rights of man, a charter expanded by the blood of generations. Those ideals still light the world, and we will not give them up for expedience's sake. And so to all other peoples and governments who are watching today, from the grandest capitals to the small village where my father was born: know that America is a friend of each nation and every man, woman, and child who seeks a future of peace and dignity, and that we are ready to lead once more.

Recall that earlier generations faced down fascism and communism not just with missiles and tanks, but with sturdy alliances and enduring convictions. They understood that our power alone cannot protect us, nor does it entitle us to do as we please. Instead, they knew that our power grows through its prudent use; our security emanates from the justness of our cause, the force of our example, the tempering qualities of humility and restraint.

We are the keepers of this legacy. Guided by these principles once more, we can meet those new threats that demand even greater effort - even greater cooperation and understanding between nations. We will begin to responsibly leave Iraq to its people, and forge a hard-earned peace in Afghanistan. With old friends and former foes, we will work tirelessly to lessen the nuclear threat, and roll back the specter of a warming planet. We will not apologize for our way of life, nor will we waver in its defense, and for those who seek to advance their aims by inducing terror and slaughtering innocents, we say to you now that our spirit is stronger and cannot be broken; you cannot outlast us, and we will defeat you.

For we know that our patchwork heritage is a strength, not a weakness. We are a nation of Christians and Muslims, Jews and Hindus - and non-believers. We are shaped by every language and culture, drawn from every end of this Earth; and because we have tasted the bitter swill of civil war and segregation, and emerged from that dark chapter stronger and more united, we cannot help but believe that the old hatreds shall someday pass; that the lines of tribe shall soon dissolve; that as the world grows smaller, our common humanity shall reveal itself; and that America must play its role in ushering in a new era of peace.

To the Muslim world, we seek a new way forward, based on mutual interest and mutual respect. To those leaders around the globe who seek to sow conflict, or blame their society's ills on the West - know that your people will judge you on what you can build, not what you destroy. To those who cling to power through corruption and deceit and the silencing of dissent, know that you are on the wrong side of history; but that we will extend a hand if you are willing to unclench your fist.

To the people of poor nations, we pledge to work alongside you to make your farms flourish and let clean waters flow; to nourish starved bodies and feed hungry minds. And to those nations like ours that enjoy relative plenty, we say we can no longer afford indifference to suffering outside our borders; nor can we consume the world's resources without regard to effect. For the world has changed, and we must change with it.

As we consider the road that unfolds before us, we remember with humble gratitude those brave Americans who, at this very hour, patrol far-off deserts and distant mountains. They have something to tell us today, just as the fallen heroes who lie in Arlington whisper through the ages. We honor them not only because they are guardians of our liberty, but because they embody the spirit of service; a willingness to find meaning in something greater than themselves. And yet, at this moment - a moment that will define a generation - it is precisely this spirit that must inhabit us all.

For as much as government can do and must do, it is ultimately the faith and determination of the American people upon which this nation relies. It is the kindness to take in a stranger when the levees break, the selflessness of workers who would rather cut their hours than see a friend lose their job which sees us through our darkest hours. It is the firefighter's courage to storm a stairway filled with smoke, but also a parent's willingness to nurture a child, that finally decides our fate.

Our challenges may be new. The instruments with which we meet them may be new. But those values upon which our success depends - hard work and honesty, courage and fair play, tolerance and curiosity, loyalty and patriotism - these things are old. These things are true. They have been the quiet force of progress throughout our history. What is demanded then is a return to these truths. What is required of us now is a new era of responsibility - a recognition, on the part of every American, that we have duties to ourselves, our nation, and the world, duties that we do not grudgingly accept but rather seize gladly, firm in the knowledge that there is nothing so satisfying to the spirit, so defining of our character, than giving our all to a difficult task.

This is the price and the promise of citizenship.

This is the source of our confidence - the knowledge that God calls on us to shape an uncertain destiny.

This is the meaning of our liberty and our creed - why men and women and children of every race and every faith can join in celebration across this magnificent mall, and why a man whose father less than sixty years ago might not have been served at a local restaurant can now stand before you to take a most sacred oath.

So let us mark this day with remembrance, of who we are and how far we have traveled. In the year of America's birth, in the coldest of months, a small band of patriots huddled by dying campfires on the shores of an icy river. The capital was abandoned. The enemy was advancing. The snow was stained with blood. At a moment when the outcome of our revolution was most in doubt, the father of our nation ordered these words be read to the people:

"Let it be told to the future world...that in the depth of winter, when nothing but hope and virtue could survive...that the city and the country, alarmed at one common danger, came forth to meet it."

America. In the face of our common dangers, in this winter of our hardship, let us remember these timeless words. With hope and virtue, let us brave once more the icy currents, and endure what storms may come. Let it be said by our children's children that when we were tested we refused to let this journey end, that we did not turn back nor did we falter; and with eyes fixed on the horizon and God's grace upon us, we carried forth that great gift of freedom and delivered it safely to future generations.

773528

Printed in Great Britain by
Amazon.co.uk, Ltd.,
Marston Gate.